The Leading Edge

Applied Insight

4

Departments

This Quarter

Picture This

On Our Web Site

Enduring Ideas

Letters to the Editor

This Quarter

Putting behavioral economics to work

Unless this issue of the *Quarterly* has made its way into Mr. Spock's hands on the bridge of the starship *Enterprise*, everyone reading it will agree that we do not make calculated, rational decisions all the time. Time pressure, uncertainty, and simple pragmatism lead us to base many decisions on our judgment. We decide with our head, but also with our gut—and for good reason.

That obvious but largely unstated fact has profound implications for the way we manage companies. This issue of the *Quarterly* views those implications through the lens of behavioral economics—a field that highlights the limits of rationality and has gained traction among practitioners in areas ranging from finance and marketing to public policy.

The application of behavioral economics to strategic decision making has been more limited, and it is this gap that the issue's cover package seeks to address. The approach to strategy formulation that we propose is based on a strikingly simple premise: since strategic decisions are made by human beings, and since human beings are subject to known, inescapable biases, companies should recognize these biases rather than ignore them and should engineer strategy formulation processes that mitigate their effects. We call this approach *behavioral strategy* and describe a number of techniques companies can employ to adopt it. Then three prominent executives—Sir Martin Sorrell, Randy Komisar, and Anne

Mulcahy—candidly discuss their decision-making styles and how they have designed decision-making processes to their advantage—but also warn readers about the risks of "overengineering" those processes. Finally, Nobel laureate Daniel Kahneman and cognitive psychologist Gary Klein debate a question that is part science, part philosophy, but all business: "When can you trust your gut?"

Of course, behavioral economics, and the growing understanding of human psychology that underlies it, have found applications across the whole spectrum of business. Elsewhere in this issue are practical tips for marketers intent on understanding consumer biases, a case study on using behavioral science to improve the customer experience in service operations, and an interview with Stanford's Chip Heath on the behavioral science of change management.

We hope this issue leaves you with a more rational view of how irrational we can all be at times and of how to turn this inescapable reality to your advantage.

Olivier Sibony
Director, Brussels office

Sven Smit
Director, Amsterdam office

8

→ On Our Web Site

Now available on
mckinseyquarterly.com

**Interactives
and videos**

Reshaping business education in a new era

Blair Sheppard, dean of Duke University's Fuqua School of Business, discusses how the expectations of MBA students are changing—and why the traditional MBA education needs to change as well.

How inflation can destroy shareholder value

An interactive slideshow displays how much a company's earnings must increase over time in order to keep cash flow stable.

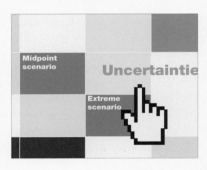

What's next for global banks

The interactive exhibit in this article explores economic and regulatory uncertainties for banks under two scenarios.

Articles

The path to successful new products

Businesses with the best product-development track records stand apart from their less successful peers in three crucial ways.

The five attributes of enduring family businesses

The keys to long-term success are professional management and keeping the family committed to and capable of carrying on as the owner.

Data to dollars: Supporting top management with next-generation executive information systems

Chief information officers have a chance to expand their influence as the mediators between business requirements and IT capabilities.

A new look at carbon offsets

Carbon markets will continue to play a role in pricing—and limiting—emissions, but the opportunity in developing markets may be less promising than once expected.

Conversation starter

Planning for your next CEO

CEO succession must be an ongoing process, not a one-time event. The company that waits to find its next CEO only when it realizes it will need one is shortchanging itself, its shareholders, and its future.

Put our headlines on your page

Our widgets allow you to share the latest *Quarterly* headlines on your social network, blog, or personalized page. Show all headlines or just those for a single function. **mckinseyquarterly.com/widgets**

Survey results

What worked in cost cutting—and what's next: McKinsey Global Survey results

Companies were able to cut costs effectively through the crisis, executives say, but they're less confident of their ability to contain or continue to cut them. Some companies are positioning themselves for longer-term success by planning the next round more strategically.

Building organizational capabilities: McKinsey Global Survey results

Building organizational capabilities, such as leadership development or lean operations, is a top priority for most companies. However, many of them have not yet figured out how to do so effectively. The odds improve at companies where senior leaders are more involved.

More from McKinsey

Join the conversation on *What Matters*

Can social entrepreneurs achieve impact at scale?

Join this discussion at: **whatmatters.mckinseydigital.com**

McKinsey's *What Matters* features both outside experts and McKinsey principals exploring the key business and social issues of our time. The latest topic: social entrepreneurs. These innovative philanthropists have crafted new responses to intractable problems, but can they have an impact on a large scale? We've convened leading thinkers and practitioners from around the world to offer their views. Read more and join the conversation on *What Matters*.

Video and audio podcasts on iTunes

Download conversations with executives and authors in audio or video from iTunes.

mckinseyquarterly.com/itunes

Recent podcasts:
A look into the future for global banks

Sector-based policy insights on growth and competitiveness

When virtual-world capabilities meet real-world business

Join the *McKinsey Quarterly* community on Facebook

facebook.com/mckinseyquarterly

Follow us on Twitter

Receive notification of new articles by following **@McKQuarterly** on Twitter.

Letters to the Editor

Reader responses to
articles in *McKinsey Quarterly*,
2010 Number 1

A new segmentation for electric vehicles

Many carmakers design electric vehicles intended to satisfy the needs of almost all customers. Instead, they should match a car's energy storage requirements to a consumer's particular needs.

The article portrays a new way to segment the market. However, the economics of car manufacturing may lead to a different scenario. The OEMs may continue to manufacture cars based on their current, traditional segmentation while entrepreneurs come up with a new business model for battery rental that allows consumers to rent battery packs depending on their needs— smaller batteries for short trips and larger ones for longer trips.

Koundinya Kammanadiminti
Senior project manager
Ford Motor Company, Dearborn, MI
USA

Manufacturers could take your proposal even further by allowing the driver to electronically select their optimum power delivery just like they can today with suspensions and transmissions. By doing this, the OEM could make all production the same, lowering costs. Then, with government funding, a progressive auto marketer could also offer flexible and multitiered lease programs tied to different lease-end residual values, depending on the percentage of vehicle miles driven in each power delivery setting.

If a customer purchases an economy lease for the cheapest cost and the vehicle spent more than 10 percent of miles on a more powerful engine-delivery setting, there would be a lease turn-in penalty just like with excess miles. This approach would give OEMs a way to standardize production while allowing governments to effectively subsidize efficient driving without calling it a personal tax. This approach could work very well to improve electronic vehicle

acceptance—however, the same approach could work for gasoline and hybrid vehicles as well. Thinking like this would be much more effective than "cash for clunkers."

Eric Conn
Consultant
VW Motorsport, Auburn Hills, MI
USA

Sorry, guys, but these findings represent nothing new. Smart did it nearly 10 years ago and, as a result of weight and range issues, decided not to further pursue a battery-powered model. Unfortunately, I have come to believe that a vehicle purchase is not a rational decision but rather an expression of freedom, lifestyle, and status. If this is true, a successful electric vehicle will have to overcome a much bigger hurdle than technology— namely, the central role of conspicuous wealth (specifically, status) in our culture. Only the increased social status associated with electric vehicles—rather than range, power, efficiency, or other attributes—will lead to a near-term breakthrough.

Richard Chrenko
Consultant
Clean tech commercialization, Bern, Switzerland

Segmenting vehicles based on mission is conceptually solid but requires a "support system" comprising either rapid-charging infrastructure or a battery-rental service model for success.

Most auto owners expect their autos to be capable of meeting a range of travel needs, even if such capability

Visit our Web site at mckinseyquarterly.com to read comments from our readers on these and other articles—or share your own.

is rarely tested or used. For example, families will likely want the soccer mom's SUV or minivan to be capable of serving the "vacation trip" mission during the holidays. This is possible through one of two approaches.

1. A battery-rental model supported with modular car designs that allow consumers to quickly add or remove battery storage depending on their mission. This approach assumes the rental provider can find adequate return from batteries that are not in use by commuters during week-ends. This model is being tested by Better Place and Nissan, in Israel.

2. Installing numerous rapid-charge facilities alongside freeways, capable of recharging batteries in 10 minutes or less. With the deployment of level-2 and -3 rapid-charge technologies, this approach could arguably trump the rental model.

However, for that to happen, consum-ers must begin to see upfront investments in the rapid-charging

infrastructure, which is only possible through coordinated efforts and investments by cities, electricity providers, and auto manufacturers.

Ojesh Bhalla
Vice president of strategy
Reliant Energy, Houston, TX USA

I must take issue with the assertion that for gas-fueled vehicles, a larger gas tank is virtually free. Within the current economic and regulatory environment, I believe quite the con-trary is true. The extra weight and packaging space required to accommodate a larger tank makes each additional gallon quite significant in cost. I understand and agree with the sizeable expense of additional batteries for the extended range and usage that you mention, but I think the reference to gas-powered vehicles' fuel tank size is over simplified.

John Whiteman
Senior advanced product planner
Honda R&D Americas, Los Angeles, CA USA

Navigating the new normal:
A conversation with four chief strategy officers

Executives of Boeing, Estée Lauder, Smith International, and Visa discuss setting strategy in the wake of the downturn.

One comment I have is how much these strategists appear to be looking inward rather than outward, which I think is more a concern of operations than strategy. I'd be more interested in what they see as the driving forces in their market places—such as consumer fear—rather than actions resulting from that fear, like a switch from credit to debit cards.

Joan McClusky
Writer
New York, NY USA

A point not covered is consumer resistance to change and the very short memories people have (particularly Americans) regarding incorporating long-lasting changes in purchasing behaviors. Most will simply return to old habits once economic conditions allow it. Maybe it would seem too crass to have mentioned that, but no doubt their companies are counting on that amidst other strategic assumptions.

Gery Sasko
President
IntraFocus Management Consulting
Chester Springs, PA USA

The Leading Edge

Research, trends, and emerging thinking

The looming deleveraging challenge

Susan Lund, Charles Roxburgh, and Tony Wimmer

Several major economies are likely to face imminent deleveraging. If history is any guide, it will be a lengthy and painful process.

The specter of deleveraging has been haunting the global economy since the credit crunch reached crisis proportions in 2008. The fear: an unwinding of unsustainable debt burdens will drag down growth rates for years to come. So far, reality has been more benign, with economic growth recovering sooner than expected in some countries, even though the financial sector is still cleaning up its balance sheets and consumer demand remains weak.

New research from the McKinsey Global Institute (MGI), however, suggests that the deleveraging pro-cess may just be getting under way and is likely to exert a significant drag on GDP growth. Our study of debt and leverage[1] in ten mature and four emerging economies[2] indicates that some sectors of the economies of five countries—Canada, South Korea, Spain, the United Kingdom, and the United States—will very probably experience deleveraging.

What's more, our analysis of deleveraging episodes since 1930 shows that virtually every major financial crisis after World War II was followed by a prolonged period in which the ratio of total debt to

Susan Lund is director of research at the McKinsey Global Institute, Charles Roxburgh is a codirector of MGI and a director in McKinsey's London office, and Tony Wimmer is a consultant in the New York office.

GDP declined significantly. The one exception was Japan, whose bursting asset bubbles in the early 1990s touched off a financial crisis followed by many years when rising government debt offset deleveraging by the private sector. The "lost decade" of sluggish GDP growth that followed is a cautionary tale for policy makers hoping to somehow avoid the painful process of deleveraging.

Business executives too will face challenges: they may have to adapt to an environment in which credit is tighter and costlier and consumer spending could be slower than trend over the medium term in countries where household debt has built up. Our findings underscore the likelihood that growth will be stronger in emerging markets, which are far less leveraged, than in mature ones. To cope, companies should build the potential impact of "pockets" of deleveraging into their market outlooks.

Where deleveraging is likely today

Debt grew rapidly after 2000 in most mature economies. Although the United States is often assumed to be the most profligate borrower, by 2008 several countries—including France, South Korea, Spain, and the United Kingdom—had higher levels of debt as a percentage of GDP. Of course, such aggregate measures of leverage are not by themselves a reliable guide to the sustainability of debt. Swiss households, for

Our analysis suggests that ten sectors have a high likelihood of deleveraging.

Likelihood of deleveraging, as of Q2 2009[1]

| | Households | Corporate | | Government | Financial institutions |
		Commercial real estate[2]	All other		
Spain	High	High	High/Moderate	Low	High/Moderate
United Kingdom	High	High	Low	Low	Moderate
United States	High	High	Low	Low	Moderate
South Korea	High	Moderate	Low	Low	Moderate
Canada	High	Moderate	Low	Low	Moderate
Italy	Low	Moderate	Moderate	Moderate	Moderate
Japan	Low	Moderate	Low	Moderate	Moderate
China	Low	Low	Low	Low	Moderate

[1]Included in study but not shown: the mature economies of France, Germany, and Switzerland; the emerging economies of Brazil, India, and Russia.
[2]Includes public and private real estate–investment vehicles.

Source: McKinsey Global Institute analysis

example, have sustainably managed very high levels of leverage for a long time because they possess high levels of financial assets that can be drawn on to repay debt and because Swiss banks have conservative lending requirements.

So to gauge the likelihood of deleveraging, we took a more granular view, studying how debt and leverage have grown over time in individual sectors of 14 major economies. We assessed the sustainability of debt by considering factors such as the level and recent growth of leverage and the borrowers' debt service capacity and vulnerability to income and interest rate shocks.

Our analysis suggests that ten sectors have a high likelihood of deleveraging. In eight of the ten, very high levels of debt are linked to real-estate booms: the household sectors of Spain, the United Kingdom, the United States, and, to a lesser extent, of Canada and South Korea, as well as the commercial-real-estate sectors of Spain, the United Kingdom, and the United States. The remaining two are parts of Spain's financial and non-real-estate corporate sectors.[3]

Overall, the corporate sectors in most countries entered the crisis with lower levels of leverage than they had at the start of the decade, with the exceptions of the commercial-real-estate subsector and companies acquired through leveraged buyouts. Both of those pockets of leverage have over $1 trillion of debt, which will need to be refinanced in coming years, suggesting difficulties ahead.

What history teaches about deleveraging

To understand what deleveraging might look like going forward, we

analyzed 45 significant, historical deleveraging episodes: those in which the ratio of total debt to GDP declined for at least three consecutive years and fell by 10 percent or more. The deleveraging episodes ranged from the US Great Depression (1929–43) to Argentina's current troubles (2000–present).

In 32 of the episodes, the deleveraging process commenced after a financial crisis and followed one of four paths. Three typically occur under economic conditions that are not currently present, so they are unlikely now: high inflation, which causes deleveraging by increasing nominal GDP growth; massive default, which typically follows currency crises; and rapid economic expansion fueled by war or oil booms. The fourth—a prolonged period of austerity, or "belt tightening"—is not only the most common path, fitting 16 of the 32 deleveraging episodes that took place after a financial crisis, but also the one that seems most relevant today.

Deleveraging through belt tightening—exemplified by the US economy during the Depression years from 1934 to 1938 and by South Korea and Malaysia after the Asian financial crisis in 1997—is usually a long and difficult process that reduces the ratio of debt to GDP by about 25 percent. Credit growth in most cases slowed dramatically: in the mature economies in our sample, it averaged 17 percent annually in the ten years prior to the crisis but fell to just 4 percent during deleveraging. Real GDP typically declined in the first two to three years of deleveraging but then rebounded and grew strongly for the next four to five years while deleveraging continued.

This time could be different

While the historical record is helpful, several elements of today's environment suggest that deleveraging may start later and take longer. First, aging populations in much of the world are causing labor force participation rates to fall, which will make it more difficult than usual to jump-start and sustain GDP growth. Another complication is that the financial crisis of 2008 was global in scale, affecting the world's biggest economies—not just one or a few, as in most previous crises. Therefore, it would be very difficult for all of today's affected countries to boost net exports simultaneously, as many did in the past to support GDP expansion when credit growth was slowing and households were saving more.

Add to that problem the prospect of sharply increasing government debt relative to GDP in several major economies. According to Global Insight, US government debt will grow to 105 percent of GDP by 2012, from 60 percent in 2008;

Deleveraging through belt tightening is usually a long and difficult process that reduces the ratio of debt to GDP by about 25 percent.

Impact of deleveraging on GDP growth

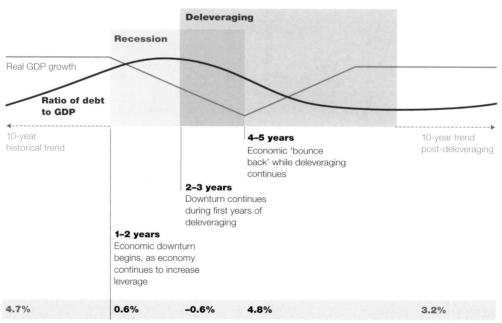

Average annual real GDP growth[1]

[1] For "belt tightening" scenario (historically, the most common path). This scenario involves a prolonged period of austerity when most countries experience some growth in credit, but at a pace far below pre-crisis rates of growth and slower than nominal GDP growth.

Source: International Monetary Fund (IMF); McKinsey Global Institute analysis

UK government debt to 91 percent, from 52 percent; and Spanish government debt to 74 percent, from 47 percent. This development could more than offset any deleveraging by the private sector. One implication is that Spain, the United Kingdom, and the United States might postpone deleveraging until after the crisis passes and growth in government debt has been reined in. It's also likely that debt-to-GDP ratios will decline more slowly and over a longer period than the historical average, creating severe headwinds on economic growth, though we do not forecast GDP.

How policy makers and business leaders can respond

Policy makers today face an acute challenge going forward. On the one hand, public policies that stimulate GDP growth will be invaluable for countries experiencing deleveraging, because such policies help an economy "grow into" its current level of debt rather than pay it off. Households and businesses can therefore save more without reducing consumption and investment as sharply as they would otherwise have to do. On the other hand, faced with rising public debt, policy makers must also carefully consider when to reduce government support of aggregate demand. Japan's experience in 1997 highlights the danger of winding down stimulus programs prematurely, potentially stifling a recovery. But it also illustrates the dangers of letting public debt grow unchecked. Getting the timing right will be critical.

Regulators are now discussing ways to improve the stability of the financial system. Our analysis strongly suggests the need for monitoring leverage at a very granular level in the real economy, since overleveraged borrowers in a few sectors were at the heart of the crisis. The data, which could then inform the banks' risk models and regulatory policies on bank capital, should be compiled at an international level, given the growth in cross-border lending and the insights that can be gleaned from cross-country comparisons. Our analysis also provides support, in principle, for a more active approach to monitoring systemic risk in the financial system.[4] We suggest caution about moves to raise bank capital ratios too quickly and too high, however, given the risk of exacerbating the pressures facing major economies as they deleverage.

Corporate executives, meanwhile, must learn to manage under con-

Japan's experience in 1997 highlights the danger of winding down stimulus programs prematurely, and of letting public debt grow unchecked

tinuing uncertainty. Business models that rely on low-cost debt will not be economically feasible, but companies with capital will find ample opportunities to expand market share or make new acquisitions. Consumer-facing businesses have already seen a shift in spending toward value-oriented goods, and this new pattern may persist until households repair their balance sheets. Scenario planning will be of the essence. We encourage business leaders to develop a range of scenarios that reflect different degrees and speeds of deleveraging rather than predicate strategies on a single view of what might unfold.

As of this writing, the deleveraging process has barely begun. Each week brings news of another country or company straining under the burden of too much debt. Deleveraging is likely to be a significant component of the post-crisis recovery, and this will dampen growth. Nevertheless, by learning lessons from past experiences of deleveraging, today's policy makers and business leaders may be better placed to steer a course through these challenging waters. ○

[1] Throughout this article, debt refers to the outstanding amount of debt, which we compared across countries by measuring it relative to GDP. Leverage, referring to debt relative to assets or income, is measured differently and often in sector-specific ways.

[2] The mature economies we examined are Canada, France, Germany, Italy, Japan, South Korea, Spain, Switzerland, the United Kingdom, and the United States. The emerging economies are Brazil, China, India, and Russia.

[3] Many countries beyond the 14 large ones in our sample increased their borrowing in the years prior to the crisis, amassing large debts relative to GDP. For small economies—particularly those that tried to build international financial hubs, such as Iceland and Ireland—the results were dramatic.

[4] Some regulators have proposed such "macroprudential" regulation—see, for example, "The role of macroprudential policy," news release by the Bank of England, November 21, 2009. Our own framework has many conceptual similarities with this but differs in several ways, including the tracking of consistent metrics across countries to enable comparisons.

For the full report, see *Debt and deleveraging: The global credit bubble and its economic consequences*, available free of charge on mckinsey.com/mgi.

Question for your COO:

Why don't back-office efficiency drives stick?

Marco Ferber, Jürgen Geiger, and Klaus Kunkel

A granular look at back-office operations shows why across-the-board cuts make no sense.

Difficult economic times are spurring many CEOs to demand cuts in corporate back offices. And no wonder: finance, HR, IT operations, and other support functions can represent 15 to 20 percent of a global company's personnel expenses and are thus prime targets for retrenchment. Yet the savings are often fleeting—we find that barely four in ten companies meet their targets one year into a cost-cutting program, and by year four fully 90 percent of back-office costs are right back where they started.

Why? One reason is that many companies pursue sweeping, top-down cuts that—while fast, easy, and seemingly fair—can unintentionally lower the effectiveness of back-office services and thereby fuel resistance among business units, many of which hire back the workers at first opportunity. To understand the risks associated with a broad-brush approach, consider the experience of a global European manufacturer's finance group, highlighted in the exhibits in this article. This snapshot of one company's situation is drawn from an ongoing proprietary benchmarking initiative that maps a range of back-office efficiency and effectiveness data at more than 900 companies in Europe and North America.[1]

A simple head count comparison suggests that the manufacturer's finance department is somewhat leaner than that of its average competitors, though about a third less lean than that of its most efficient one. Many COOs, CFOs, and other executives armed primarily with such high-level information initiate across-the-board layoffs, process improvements, or both. That's a mistake. In fact, a more granular look at the efficiency of the finance department's constituent parts (general accounting, treasury, and so on) reveals that only its revenue-management operation has a leaner head count than that of the company's average competitors. In other words, superior efficiency in one area masks moderate inefficiency throughout the rest. Across-the-board layoffs would eliminate muscle as well as fat.

Of course, efficiency is only half of the equation. To capitalize on the potential for improvement and make changes stick, executives must also consider the effectiveness of back-office services. Here too a closer look is revealing, as it suggests that the manufacturer's revenue-management operation, which takes fully twice as long as its rivals do to secure payment, is far *less* effective than its peers

Marco Ferber is an associate principal in McKinsey's Stuttgart office; Jürgen Geiger is a principal in the Düsseldorf office, where Klaus Kunkel is a consultant.

in managing receivables. Applying this lens to the rest of the company's finance group suggests that its services could be 50 percent more effective. The manufacturer's executives could use that information to begin developing more accurate—and realistic—targets for efficiency and effectiveness. Simultaneously, they could probe the root causes of these performance deficits to learn where lean and other process-improvement techniques might be advantageous.

Companies miss such opportunities when they take a hands-off approach to managing back-office complexity.

A high-level view suggested the manufacturer's finance group was more efficient than average ...

Number of full-time employees in finance department

= **5** employees

Index: industry average = **100**

Manufacturer = **94**

Best practice = **60**

...but a closer examination revealed wide variations in performance and big opportunities for improvement.

Gap between company performance and competitor average;
index: competitor average = 0

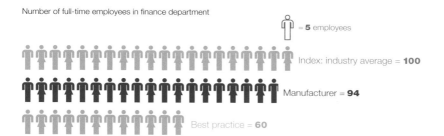

Finance subfunctions	Efficiency[1]	Effectiveness[2]
General accounting	−4	159
Revenue management	23	−51
Accounts payable	−6	−42
Financial planning	−2	−3
Treasury	−5	−5
Tax	−1	−12

Potential for improvement	**18%** in combined opportunities on the subfunctional level	**Up to 50%**—although performance varies substantially among subfunctions

[1] Efficiency is measured by the number of full-time equivalents (FTEs) for each category or subfunction.
[2] Effectiveness is measured in general accounting as lead time to close general ledger at the end of a month; in revenue management, as average number of days for receivables outstanding; in accounts payable, as average number of days for payables outstanding; in financial planning, as deviation in earnings before interest and taxes (EBIT) from plan at year end; in treasury, as relative interest rate achieved for debt; and in tax, as effective corporate tax rate.

By contrast, top companies closely monitor both the efficiency *and* the effectiveness of support activities and recognize that improvements to the former need not come at the expense of the latter (a key insight confirmed by our research). In fact, there are often interdependencies between the two. Greater effectiveness can even contribute to higher efficiency. Within the finance function, for example, paying more attention to the creditworthiness of customers and setting shorter payment cycles (effectiveness gains) help reduce the need for write-offs and make posting to accounts more straightforward (greater efficiency).

Mastering such interdependencies across the breadth of a company's back-office operations pays big dividends. If an average performer in our database raised its back-office

efficiency and effectiveness to top-quartile levels, it would improve its net margin by two percentage points. Moreover, greater transparency allows companies to make better off-shoring decisions and to integrate back-office services more closely with core businesses, improving productivity in adjacent areas— all while helping to ensure that operational improvements stick.○

[1] The data include employment figures, as well as various effectiveness metrics for 920 companies in Europe, North America, and elsewhere. The study spans a range of industries (automotive and assembly, banking, basic materials, consumer goods and services, among others) and includes all major general and administrative functions (for instance, data processing and IT, finance, HR, marketing, purchasing, and real estate). When possible, we break the functions down into subfunctions, such as employee benefits (HR) and accounts receivable (finance).

We welcome your comments on this article. Please send them to quarterly_comments@mckinsey.com.

Survey finding

44% of executives in a recent McKinsey Global survey said their companies took an across-the-board approach to cost cutting; these respondents were more likely than others to say the cuts wouldn't be sustainable

The full survey, "What worked in cost cutting—and what's next," is available on mckinseyquarterly.com.

A lighter touch for postmerger integration

David Cogman and Jacqueline Tan

Some Asian companies are taking a light-handed approach to integrating acquisitions outside their borders.

When it comes to acquisitions, some Asian companies are forging a novel path through the thicket of postmerger integration: they aren't doing it. While it's practically an article of faith among Western companies that acquirers must integrate their targets quickly or else lose momentum and fail to capture the synergies that justified the deal, McKinsey research in Asia finds that about half of all acquiring companies between 2004 and 2008 took a lighter touch. The long-term ramifications of this trend have yet to be seen, but Western executives should take note, as a better understanding of the motivations and tactics of these Asian dealmakers has implications for both the companies eyeing acquisition partners and for the strategies of buyers facing competition from Asian bidders.

These are among the conclusions from a study of 120 Asian acquisitions that were made from the beginning of 2004 through the third quarter of 2008. Contrary to common perceptions, these deals were seldom purely financial portfolio investments: all but 5 percent of those we examined had a clearly articulated commercial rationale for how they would generate synergies.[1] Yet over a third of the Asian deals

David Cogman is a principal in McKinsey's Shanghai office, and Jacqueline Tan is a consultant in the Hong Kong office.

involved only limited functional integration and focused instead on the capture of selected synergies in areas such as procurement, with an overwhelming emphasis on business stability. An additional 10 percent attempted no functional integration whatsoever. In short, many Asian acquirers aren't rushing to become hands-on managers.

So why buy a business and leave it substantially alone? The answer lies in the acquirer's priorities. In Europe and the United States, factors that influence postmerger management include the need to meet requirements for adequate internal controls as publicly listed companies, along with investor pressure to rapidly produce synergies. By contrast, many Asian acquirers feel much less pressure from capital markets—a product of less frequent reporting requirements or different ownership structures (including state control).

Many of the acquisitions we examined follow a similar model, characterized by a desire to minimize integration activity and disruption to the target:

Oversight and management: The typical acquirer aims to achieve effective oversight of its acquisitions without substituting its own judgment for that of the existing line management. For example, some create a board or supervisory committee that combines leadership from both incumbent and acquirer, along with select external appointees—much in the way a private-equity firm might restructure an acquisition's board. Similarly, many Asian acquirers, rather than inserting their own staff into key roles, build the management team of the acquired company from its incumbent executives, along with select local hires.

Focus on a few synergies: Instead of dissipating their attention across a broad portfolio of projects, managers generally focus on a few top sources of synergy such as joint sourcing, technology transfer, or cross-selling. In those select instances, acquirers often create teams made up of both their own and the acquired company's staff to examine specific synergy capture opportunities. A related point is that many Asian

acquirers take a light touch to the use of key performance indicators— and generally track a very limited set of metrics (though the amount of data monitored depends largely on the sector).

Back-office integration: It's often more limited than in a typical European or North American merger. For example, the full-scale migration of the acquirer's enterprise-resource-planning platforms is not the default option (though Asian companies do initially conduct a review of back-office functions to catch data reliability issues). When a much more limited data extraction system can generate the required management information, Asian acquirers find this approach faster, cheaper, and more likely to succeed.

Western readers might ask whether this Asian approach merely produces a transitory structure that will inevitably lead to full integration. At this stage, it's too early to tell— or to judge whether the approach

The 'Asian approach' to M&A is worth watching: the region saw more than **1,900 deals, worth $145 billion,** in 2009 alone

will, in the long run, create more or less value than a more traditional integration approach would have. Down the road, hands-off Asian acquirers may need to pursue more comprehensive integration programs, which will be more challenging as a result of the delay. Still, if such acquirers do eventually integrate successfully, they will have lowered the short-term, postacquisition risks without seriously compromising longer-term benefits.

Nonetheless, with over 1,900 total deals in the region, worth $145 billion, in 2009 alone, the trend bears watching. It may, for example, affect how companies looking to sell themselves perceive different potential acquirers; a lot of companies would prefer to sell out to a company that won't take a heavy-handed approach to sudden integration. Likewise, it might affect how a Western company thinks about potential acquisition partners—and what their integration agendas might be. It almost certainly will expand the number of bidders for assets on the block and affect bidding strategies, particularly if cost synergies are not primary considerations for acquirers who intend minimal integration. And finally, it may result in unexpected new entrants to an industry that could quickly change the competitive landscape. o

We welcome your comments on this article. Please send them to quarterly_comments@ mckinsey.com.

[1] For half of the deals, the disclosed rationale was expansion into a new market or geography, an adjacent business line, or a related business area. For a further 20 percent, it was the acquisition of a new organizational capability, and for 18 percent, access to scarce resources, vertical integration to ensure security of supply, or both.

 The full version of this article is available on mckinseyquarterly.com.

Conversation starter:

How helping women helps business

Irina A. Nikolic and Lynn Taliento

Companies whose social investments focus on women in developing economies help not only the recipients but also themselves.

Few companies make social investments specifically aimed at empowering women in developing economies, but we believe that supporting this goal is good business and good practice for all companies. In the course of our work,[1] we've uncovered a startlingly wide range of ways in which private-sector companies can offer sizable economic benefits not only to women and their societies but also to the companies themselves. The benefits to businesses come from enlarging their markets, improving the quality or size of their current and potential workforce (for instance, by attracting talent globally), and maintaining or improving their reputations.

Women in developing economies are hampered by many of the same concerns that face women in other countries, but they also deal with a number of additional barriers to economic security. In some cases, these problems are straightforward—girls getting less food and education than boys, for example. In others, they are as complicated as the difficulty women in many countries have in keeping control over money they may earn (because of regulations or long-standing cultural traditions that prevent them from having secure access to

bank accounts), owning property, or acquiring loans.

Women's unfulfilled potential significantly hinders economic growth. One recent study, for example, estimates that lower education and employment rates for women and girls are responsible for as much as a 1.6 percentage point difference in annual GDP growth between South Asia and East Asia.[2] On the other hand, educated, income-earning women are especially powerful catalysts for development because they tend to invest more of their money in their families' health, education, and well-being than men do.

Nevertheless, only 19 percent of the respondents to a recent *McKinsey Quarterly* survey said that their companies had invested in economic-development activities specifically aimed at women in developing markets. Yet 83 percent said that economic growth there was at least somewhat important to their companies' success over the next ten years.

Companies whose social investments do focus on women in developing economies, the survey and our other research show, benefit not only women and their societies but also

Irina Nikolic is an associate principal in McKinsey's Washington, DC, office, where Lynn Taliento is a principal.

themselves. Among survey respondents, 34 percent say that such investments have already improved profits, and a further 38 percent expect them to do so.

Even more notably, our research shows that private-sector companies can create such benefits with a much broader range of measures than most executives believe. Promoting literacy, for example, offers a straightforward link to improved workforce productivity—but, it turns out, so does providing antiretroviral drugs to workers' families. Anglo American, a mining company, extends HIV antiretroviral benefits to dependents (mostly women and children) of its employees in Africa. It has benefited from increased worker loyalty—retention rates are up—and from fewer missed workdays by employees who would otherwise need to care for sick family members. Furthermore, the communities Anglo American is serving now see lower infant mortality rates and healthier children.

Hindustan Lever's Shakti program, meanwhile, tapped into the significant potential of empowering women to reach markets the company couldn't otherwise. Launched in 2000, the program offers microcredit grants that enable rural women to become direct-to-home distributors of Hindustan Lever products. This new sales force has significantly boosted sales of the company's products in rural villages, a market

Comments from readers on mckinseyquarterly.com

I do not think that promoting, supporting, or developing leadership of females is a female's job. It is the responsibility of the entire company. I do not believe that terms such as "equality" should be used, as it is rather "harmonization" of the company to employees that it respects and values. I feel that somehow many men (and some women, for that matter) feel that to be successful in business they need to be mean, tough warriors. I posit that the profitable and successful organizations of the future will be the ones that have harmony. There is a time for nurturing and for destroying. The wisdom comes in knowing which one is required in each given scenario.

Zano Tyrannis
Clinic director, Back to Health
Windsor, ON, CA

My company has funded eight village banks (microfinancing programs) for women in Asia. This is one of the ways we use some of our profits to make a difference. While our staff are proud of these efforts, I don't think there is a direct relationship between these efforts and our company performance—nor does it matter to me. Results will not be seen in the short term. It's the long term that matters.

Alison Eyring
CEO, Organisation Solutions
Singapore

that is otherwise dauntingly expensive to reach. By the end of 2008, the Shakti network had grown to include more than 45,000 saleswomen covering more than 100,000 villages and more than three million homes in India.[3]

Private-sector programs can also give companies longer-term or more intangible rewards, such as maintaining a positive brand image or creating a more educated workforce or wealthier consumers. In India, Standard Chartered recently partnered with the International Federation of Netball Associations to build a program designed to use the sport to develop the life skills and self-esteem of girls between 14 and 16 years of age from families earning less than $2 a day. Piloted in Mumbai and Delhi, and currently being significantly expanded, the program includes an additional direct economic-empowerment component: a loan fund to help girls achieve their professional goals.[4]

Private-sector companies, we've found, can make development investments in programs that help girls and women throughout their lives—from infancy through education, preparation for work, support in the workplace, and ensuring financial security. For each stage of women's lives, we've distilled

EGMM is the jobs mission of the Andhra Pradesh government, which invests in identifying youth, skilling them up in short-term, market-linked courses and linking them to jobs. Set up five years back, the focus of the work is to get the vulnerable children—specifically, girls—into the program. This stems from our firm belief that investing in a girl means impacting the family and a new generation. Initially, there were many challenges ranging from parents wanting to get their daughters married early to families preferring girls to remain at home and help with housework. By sensitizing the mothers of the girls, today 51 percent of our youth in jobs are girls. A father (a shepherd by profession) of one of our alumni told me, "We considered her birth a curse. Today she is bringing prestige to our family."

Meera Shenoy
Executive director, EGMM
Hyderabad, India

It is encouraging to see that statistics and data support our long-time belief that empowering women and girls leads to long-term prosperity and economic growth. Harnessing women's talents and enabling their realization of potential is not only good business, but smart business.

Wenchi Yu
Policy adviser, US Department of State
Washington, DC, USA

a set of high-impact actions, which range from offering prenatal care and infant vaccinations to providing onsite bank accounts ensuring that female employees control their income and retirement savings. Companies don't have to go it alone: successful ones, we've seen, design and implement their investments collaboratively with the women they're trying to help, nongovernmental organizations with relevant experience, and other companies with similar interests. They can create real benefits for everyone by creatively combining an interest in empowering women in developing markets with a strategic assessment of where doing so can help meet corporate goals. o

[1] Our full report, *The business of empowering women*, is available free of charge on mckinsey.com.

[2] Stephan Klasen and Francesca Lamanna, *The Impact of Gender Inequality in Education and Employment on Economic Growth in Developing Countries: Updates and Extensions*, Ibero-America Institute for Economic Research (IAI) discussion paper 175, Ibero-America Institute for Economic Research, 2008.

[3] See V. Kasturi Rangan and Rohithari Rajan, "Unilever in India: Hindustan Lever's Project Shakti – Marketing FMCG to the rural consumer," Harvard Business School Case 9-505-056, 2007; and also Hindustan Lever annual report, 2008.

[4] Bill Wilson, "Netball aims to change Indian lives," *BBC News*, May 20, 2009.

Businesses that continue to look at the world and their markets through a 'male-centric' perspective will likely overlook certain types of talent, trends, and needs that a broader perspective would not. Anyone who is deeply enmeshed in a monoculture tends to be blinded by their own culture. A pluri-culture (such as men and women) is more likely to uncover blind spots.

Sabine Amend
Executive director, Kultur & Management
Longmont, CO, USA

Where corporate initiatives fill the gap in delivery of education, health, and social services usually expected of government, they are always well received by benefiting communities and generate good will. Whether they advance the interests of the corporate sponsor is dependent on the program structure. The Shakti program delivers what it is designed to do, namely, to develop direct-marketing services for household consumables through the medium of trained women. Investments in primary education and adolescent health are less geared to deliver direct benefit to sponsoring companies. To draw a direct connection between female literacy, maternal health, etcetera, and sponsoring-company profits is, I believe, a bit of a stretch.

Shailaja Sharma
Manager, *Shell India*
New Delhi, India

 The full version of this article is available on mckinseyquarterly.com.

On the cover

Seeing through biases in strategic decisions

Artwork by Paul Wearing

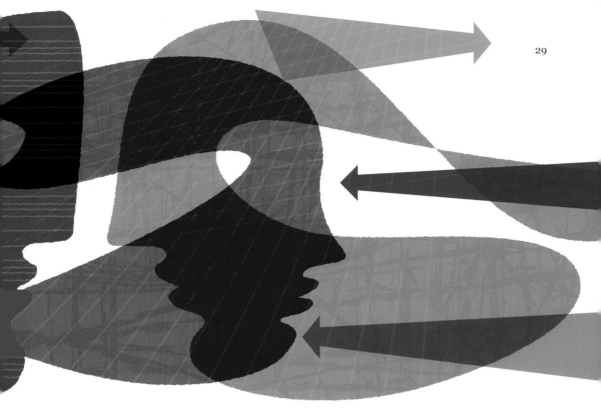

The case
for behavioral
strategy

Dan Lovallo and Olivier Sibony

Left unchecked, subconscious biases will undermine strategic decision making. Here's how to counter them and improve corporate performance.

Dan Lovallo is a professor at the University of Sydney, a senior research fellow at the Institute for Business Innovation at the University of California, Berkeley, and an adviser to McKinsey; Olivier Sibony is a director in McKinsey's Brussels office.

Once heretical, behavioral economics is now mainstream. Money managers employ its insights about the limits of rationality in understanding investor behavior and exploiting stock-pricing anomalies. Policy makers use behavioral principles to boost participation in retirement-savings plans. Marketers now understand why some promotions entice consumers and others don't.

Yet very few corporate strategists making important decisions consciously take into account the cognitive biases—systematic tendencies to deviate from rational calculations—revealed by behavioral economics. It's easy to see why: unlike in fields such as finance and marketing, where executives can use psychology to make the most

of the biases residing in *others*, in strategic decision making leaders need to recognize *their own* biases. So despite growing awareness of behavioral economics and numerous efforts by management writers, including ourselves, to make the case for its application, most executives have a justifiably difficult time knowing how to harness its power.[1]

This is not to say that executives think their strategic decisions are perfect. In a recent *McKinsey Quarterly* survey of 2,207 executives, only 28 percent said that the quality of strategic decisions in their companies was generally good, 60 percent thought that bad decisions were about as frequent as good ones, and the remaining 12 percent thought good decisions were altogether infrequent.[2] Our candid conversations with senior executives behind closed doors reveal a similar unease with the quality of decision making and confirm the significant body of research indicating that cognitive biases affect the most important strategic decisions made by the smartest managers in the best companies. Mergers routinely fail to deliver the expected synergies.[3] Strategic plans often ignore competitive responses.[4] And large investment projects are over budget and over time—over and over again.[5]

In this article, we share the results of new research quantifying the financial benefits of processes that "debias" strategic decisions. The size of this prize makes a strong case for practicing behavioral strategy—a style of strategic decision making that incorporates the lessons of psychology. It starts with the recognition that even if we try, like Baron Münchhausen, to escape the swamp of biases by pulling ourselves up by our own hair, we are unlikely to succeed. Instead, we need new norms for activities such as managing meetings (for more on running unbiased meetings, see pp. 68–69), gathering data, discussing analogies, and stimulating debate that together can diminish the impact of cognitive biases on critical decisions. To support those new norms, we also need a simple language for recognizing and discussing biases, one that is grounded in the reality of corporate life, as opposed to the sometimes-arcane language of academia. All this represents a significant commitment and, in some organizations, a profound cultural change.

[1] See Charles Roxburgh, "Hidden flaws in strategy," mckinseyquarterly.com, May 2003; and Dan P. Lovallo and Olivier Sibony, "Distortions and deceptions in strategic decisions," mckinseyquarterly.com, February 2006.
[2] See "Flaws in strategic decision making: McKinsey Global Survey Results," mckinseyquarterly.com, January 2009.
[3] See Dan Lovallo, Patrick Viguerie, Robert Uhlaner, and John Horn, "Deals without delusions," *Harvard Business Review,* December 2007, Volume 85, Number 12, pp. 92–99.
[4] See John T. Horn, Dan P. Lovallo, and S. Patrick Viguerie, "Beating the odds in market entry," mckinseyquarterly.com, November 2005.
[5] See Bent Flyvbjerg, Dan Lovallo, and Massimo Garbuio, "Delusion and deception in large infrastructure projects," *California Management Review,* 2009, Volume 52, Number 1, pp. 170–93.

What we did

1,048 Number of decisions analyzed

76% Share of decisions related to M&A, organizational change, or expansion into new geographies, products, and services

51% Proportion of decisions that could be attributed to a single, specific business function (sales, R&D, marketing, manufacturing, or supply chain/distribution)

The value of good decision processes

Think of a large business decision your company made recently: a major acquisition, a large capital expenditure, a key technological choice, or a new-product launch. Three things went into it. The decision almost certainly involved some fact gathering and analysis. It relied on the insights and judgment of a number of executives (a number sometimes as small as one). And it was reached after a process—sometimes very formal, sometimes completely informal—turned the data and judgment into a decision.

Our research indicates that, contrary to what one might assume, good analysis in the hands of managers who have good judgment won't naturally yield good decisions. The third ingredient—the process— is also crucial. We discovered this by asking managers to report on both the nature of an important decision and the process through which it was reached. In all, we studied 1,048 major decisions made over the past five years, including investments in new products, M&A decisions, and large capital expenditures.

Process, analysis, and industry variables explain decision-making effectiveness

Share of performance explained by given element
(based on multivariate regression analysis), %

Quantity and detail of analysis performed—eg, detailed financial modeling, sensitivity analysis, analysis of financial reaction of markets

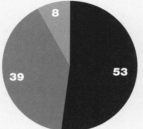

Industry/company variables—eg, number of investment opportunities, capital availability, predictability of consumer tastes, availability of resources to implement decision

Quality of process to exploit analysis and reach decision—eg, explicit exploration of major uncertainties, inclusion of perspectives that contradict senior leader's point of view, allowing participation in discussion by skill and experience rather than by rank

Note: To evaluate decision-making effectiveness, we asked respondents to assess outcomes along four dimensions: revenue, profitability, market share, and productivity.

We asked managers to report on the extent to which they had applied 17 practices in making that decision. Eight of these practices had to do with the quantity and detail of the analysis: did you, for example, build a detailed financial model or run sensitivity analyses? The others described the decision-making process: for instance, did you explicitly explore and discuss major uncertainties or discuss viewpoints that contradicted the senior leader's? We chose these process characteristics because in academic research and in our experience, they have proved effective at overcoming biases.[6]

After controlling for factors like industry, geography, and company size, we used regression analysis to calculate how much of the variance in decision outcomes[7] was explained by the quality of the process and

[6] Research like this is challenging because of what International Institute for Management Development (IMD) professor Phil Rosenzweig calls the "halo effect": the tendency of people to believe that when their companies are successful or a decision turns out well, their actions were important contributors (see Phil Rosenzweig, "The halo effect, and other managerial delusions," mckinseyquarterly.com, February 2007). We sought to mitigate the halo effect by asking respondents to focus on a typical decision process in their companies and to list several decisions before landing on one for detailed questioning. Next, we asked analytical and process questions about the specific decision for the bulk of the survey. Finally, at the very end of it, we asked about performance metrics.

[7] We asked respondents to assess outcomes along four dimensions: revenue, profitability, market share, and productivity.

Difference in ROI between top- and bottom-quartile decision inputs, percentage points

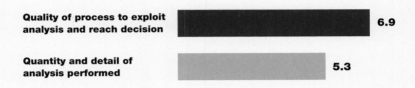

Quality of process to exploit
analysis and reach decision   6.9

Quantity and detail of
analysis performed   5.3

how much by the quantity and detail of the analysis. The answer: process mattered more than analysis—by a factor of six. This finding does not mean that analysis is unimportant, as a closer look at the data reveals: almost no decisions in our sample made through a very strong process were backed by very poor analysis. Why? Because one of the things an unbiased decision-making process will do is ferret out poor analysis. The reverse is not true; superb analysis is useless unless the decision process gives it a fair hearing.

To get a sense of the value at stake, we also assessed the return on investment (ROI) of decisions characterized by a superior process.[8] The analysis revealed that raising a company's game from the bottom to the top quartile on the decision-making process improved its ROI by 6.9 percentage points. The ROI advantage for top-quartile versus bottom-quartile analytics was 5.3 percentage points, further underscoring the tight relationship between process and analysis. Good process, in short, isn't just good hygiene; it's good business.

[8]This analysis covers the subset of 673 (out of all 1,048) decisions for which ROI data were available.

The building blocks of behavioral strategy

Any seasoned executive will of course recognize some biases and take them into account. That is what we do when we apply a discount factor to a plan from a direct report (correcting for that person's overoptimism). That is also what we do when we fear that one person's recommendation may be colored by self-interest and ask a neutral third party for an independent opinion.

However, academic research and empirical observation suggest that these corrections are too inexact and limited to be helpful. The prevalence of biases in corporate decisions is partly a function of habit, training, executive selection, and corporate culture. But most fundamentally, biases are pervasive because they are a product of human nature—hard-wired and highly resistant to feedback, however brutal. For example, drivers laid up in hospitals for traffic accidents they themselves caused overestimate their driving abilities just as much as the rest of us do.[9]

Improving strategic decision making therefore requires not only trying to limit our own (and others') biases but also orchestrating a decision-making process that will confront different biases and limit their impact. To use a judicial analogy, we cannot trust the judges or the jurors to be infallible; they are, after all, human. But as citizens, we can expect verdicts to be rendered by juries and trials to follow the rules of due process. It is through teamwork, and the process that organizes it, that we seek a high-quality outcome.

Building such a process for strategic decision making requires an understanding of the biases the process needs to address. In the discussion that follows, we focus on the subset of biases we have found to be most relevant for executives and classify those biases into five simple, business-oriented groupings (for more on these groupings, see pp. 44–45). A familiarity with this classification is useful in itself because, as the psychologist and Nobel laureate in economics Daniel Kahneman has pointed out, the odds of defeating biases in a group setting rise when discussion of them is widespread. But familiarity alone isn't enough to ensure unbiased decision making, so as we discuss each family of bias, we also provide some general principles and specific examples of practices that can help counteract it.

Counter pattern-recognition biases by changing the angle of vision

The ability to identify patterns helps set humans apart but also carries with it a risk of misinterpreting conceptual relationships. Common

---

[9] Caroline E. Preston and Stanley Harris, "Psychology of drivers in traffic accidents," *Journal of Applied Psychology,* 1965, Volume 49, Number 4, pp. 284–88.

In most organizations, an executive who projects great confidence in a plan is more likely to get it approved than one who lays out all the risks and uncertainties surrounding it

pattern-recognition biases include saliency biases (which lead us to overweight recent or highly memorable events) and the confirmation bias (the tendency, once a hypothesis has been formed, to ignore evidence that would disprove it). Particularly imperiled are senior executives, whose deep experience boosts the odds that they will rely on analogies, from their own experience, that may turn out to be misleading.[10] Whenever analogies, comparisons, or salient examples are used to justify a decision, and whenever convincing champions use their powers of persuasion to tell a compelling story, pattern-recognition biases may be at work.

Pattern recognition is second nature to all of us—and often quite valuable—so fighting biases associated with it is challenging. The best we can do is to change the angle of vision by encouraging participants to see facts in a different light and to test alternative hypotheses to explain those facts. This practice starts with things as simple as field and customer visits. It continues with meeting-management techniques such as reframing or role reversal, which encourage participants to formulate alternative explanations for the evidence with which they are presented. It can also leverage tools, such as competitive war games, that promote out-of-the-box thinking.

Sometimes, simply coaxing managers to articulate the experiences influencing them is valuable. According to Kleiner Perkins partner Randy Komisar, for example, a contentious discussion over manufacturing strategy at the start-up WebTV [11] suddenly became much more manageable once it was clear that the preferences of executives about which strategy to pursue stemmed from their previous career

[10] For more on misleading experiences, see Sydney Finkelstein, Jo Whitehead, and Andrew Campbell, *Think Again: Why Good Leaders Make Bad Decisions and How to Keep It from Happening to You,* Boston: Harvard Business Press, 2008.
[11] WebTV is now MSN TV.

experience. When that realization came, he told us, there was immediately a "sense of exhaling in the room." Managers with software experience were frightened about building hardware; managers with hardware experience were afraid of ceding control to contract manufacturers.

Getting these experiences into the open helped WebTV's management team become aware of the pattern recognition they triggered and see more clearly the pros and cons of both options. Ultimately, WebTV's executives decided both to outsource hardware production to large electronics makers and, heeding the worries of executives with hardware experience, to establish a manufacturing line in Mexico as a backup, in case the contractors did not deliver in time for the Christmas season. That in fact happened, and the backup plan, which would not have existed without a decision process that changed the angle of vision, "saved the company."

Another useful means of changing the angle of vision is to make it wider by creating a reasonably large—in our experience at least six—set of similar endeavors for comparative analysis. For example, in an effort to improve US military effectiveness in Iraq in 2004, Colonel Kalev Sepp—by himself, in 36 hours—developed a reference class of 53 similar counterinsurgency conflicts, complete with strategies and outcomes. This effort informed subsequent policy changes.[12]

Counter action-oriented biases by recognizing uncertainty

Most executives rightly feel a need to take action. However, the actions we take are often prompted by excessive optimism about the future and especially about our own ability to influence it. Ask yourself how many plans you have reviewed that turned out to be based on overly optimistic forecasts of market potential or underestimated competitive responses. When you or your people feel—especially under pressure—an urge to take action and an attractive plan presents itself, chances are good that some elements of overconfidence have tainted it.

To make matters worse, the culture of many organizations suppresses uncertainty and rewards behavior that ignores it. For instance, in most organizations, an executive who projects great confidence in a plan is more likely to get it approved than one who lays out all the risks and uncertainties surrounding it. Seldom do we see confidence as a warning sign—a hint that overconfidence, overoptimism, and other action-oriented biases may be at work.

Superior decision-making processes counteract action-oriented biases by promoting the recognition of uncertainty. For example, it often

---

[12] Thomas E. Ricks, *Fiasco: The American Military Adventure in Iraq*, New York: Penguin Press, 2006, pp. 393–94.

helps to make a clear and explicit distinction between decision meetings, where leaders should embrace uncertainty while encouraging dissent, and implementation meetings, where it's time for executives to move forward together. Also valuable are tools—such as scenario planning, decision trees, and the "premortem" championed by research psychologist Gary Klein (for more on the premortem, see p. 64)—that force consideration of many potential outcomes. And at the time of a major decision, it's critical to discuss which metrics need to be monitored to highlight necessary course corrections quickly.

Counter stability biases by shaking things up

In contrast to action biases, stability biases make us less prone to depart from the status quo than we should be. This category includes anchoring—the powerful impact an initial idea or number has on the subsequent strategic conversation. (For instance, last year's numbers are an implicit but extremely powerful anchor in any budget review.) Stability biases also include loss aversion—the well-documented tendency to feel losses more acutely than equivalent gains—and the sunk-cost fallacy, which can lead companies to hold on to businesses they should divest.[13]

One way of diagnosing your company's susceptibility to stability biases is to compare decisions over time. For example, try mapping the percentage of total new investment each division of the company receives year after year. If that percentage is stable but the divisions' growth opportunities are not, this finding is cause for concern—and quite a common one. Our research indicates, for example, that in multi-business corporations over a 15-year time horizon, there is a near-perfect correlation between a business unit's current share of the capital expenditure budget and its budget share in the previous year. A similar inertia often bedevils advertising budgets and R&D project pipelines.

One way to help managers shake things up is to establish stretch targets that are impossible to achieve through "business as usual." Zero-based (or clean-sheet) budgeting sounds promising, but in our experience companies use this approach only when they are in dire straits. An alternative is to start by reducing each reporting unit's budget by a fixed percentage (for instance, 10 percent). The resulting tough choices facilitate the redeployment of resources to more valuable opportunities. Finally, challenging budget allocations at a more granular level can help companies reprioritize their investments.[14]

[13] See John T. Horn, Dan P. Lovallo, and S. Patrick Viguerie, "Learning to let go: Making better exit decisions," mckinseyquarterly.com, May 2006.
[14] For more on reviewing the growth opportunities available across different micromarkets ranging in size from $50 million to $200 million, rather than across business units as a whole, see Mehrdad Baghai, Sven Smit, and Patrick Viguerie, "Is your growth strategy flying blind?" *Harvard Business Review,* May 2009, Volume 87, Number 5, pp. 86–96.

Counter interest biases by making them explicit

Misaligned incentives are a major source of bias. "Silo thinking," in which organizational units defend their own interests, is its most easily detectable manifestation. Furthermore, senior executives sometimes honestly view the goals of a company differently because of their different roles or functional expertise. Heated discussions in which participants seem to see issues from completely different perspectives often reflect the presence of different (and generally unspoken) interest biases.

The truth is that adopting a sufficiently broad (and realistic) definition of "interests," including reputation, career options, and individual preferences, leads to the inescapable conclusion that there will always be conflicts between one manager and another and between individual managers and the company as a whole. Strong decision-making processes explicitly account for diverging interests. For example, if before the time of a decision, strategists formulate precisely the criteria that will and won't be used to evaluate it, they make it more difficult for individual managers to change the terms of the debate to make their preferred actions seem more attractive. Similarly, populating meetings or teams with participants whose interests clash can reduce the likelihood that one set of interests will undermine thoughtful decision making.

Counter social biases by depersonalizing debate

Social biases are sometimes interpreted as corporate politics but in fact are deep-rooted human tendencies. Even when nothing is at stake, we tend to conform to the dominant views of the group we belong to (and of its leader).[15] Many organizations compound these tendencies because of both strong corporate cultures and incentives to conform. An absence of dissent is a strong warning sign. Social biases also are likely to prevail in discussions where everyone in the room knows the views of the ultimate decision maker (and assumes that the leader is unlikely to change her mind).

Countless techniques exist to stimulate debate among executive teams, and many are simple to learn and practice. (For more on promoting debate, see suggestions from Kleiner Perkins' Randy Komisar on pp. 50–51, as well as from Xerox's Anne Mulcahy on pp. 55–56.) But tools per se won't create debate: that is a matter of behavior. Genuine debate requires diversity in the backgrounds and personalities of the decision makers, a climate of trust, and a culture in which discussions are depersonalized.

---

[15] The Asch conformity experiments, conducted during the 1950s, are a classic example of this dynamic. In the experiments, individuals gave clearly incorrect answers to simple questions after confederates of the experimenter gave the same incorrect answers aloud. See Solomon E. Asch, "Opinions and social pressure," *Scientific American*, 1955, Volume 193, Number 5, pp. 31–35.

Populating meetings or teams with participants whose interests clash can reduce the likelihood that one set of interests will undermine thoughtful decision making

Most crucially, debate calls for senior leaders who genuinely believe in the collective intelligence of a high-caliber management team. Such executives see themselves serving not only as the ultimate decision makers but also as the orchestrators of disciplined decision processes. They shape management teams with the humility to encourage dissent and the self-confidence and mutual trust to practice vigorous debate without damaging personal relationships. We do not suggest that CEOs should become humble listeners who rely solely on the consensus of their teams—that would substitute one simplistic stereotype for another. But we do believe that behavioral strategy will founder without their leadership and role modeling.

Four steps to adopting behavioral strategy

Our readers will probably recognize some of these ideas and tools as techniques they have used in the past. But techniques by themselves will not improve the quality of decisions. Nothing is easier, after all, than orchestrating a perfunctory debate to justify a decision already made (or thought to be made) by the CEO. Leaders who want to shape the decision-making style of their companies must commit themselves to a new path.

1

Decide which decisions warrant the effort

Some executives fear that applying the principles we describe here could be divisive, counterproductive, or simply too time consuming (for more on the dangers of decision paralysis, see the commentary by WPP's Sir Martin Sorrell on p. 47). We share this concern and do not suggest applying these principles to all decisions. Here again, the judicial analogy is instructive. Just as higher standards of process apply in a capital case than in a proceeding before a small-claims court, companies can and should pay special attention to two types of decisions.

The first set consists of rare, one-of-a-kind strategic decisions. Major mergers and acquisitions, "bet the company" investments, and crucial technological choices fall in this category. In most companies, these decisions are made by a small subgroup of the executive team, using an ad hoc, informal, and often iterative process. The second set includes repetitive but high-stakes decisions that shape a company's strategy over time. In most companies, there are generally no more than one or two such crucial processes, such as R&D allocations in a pharmaceutical company, investment decisions in a private-equity firm, or capital expenditure decisions in a utility. Formal processes—often affected by biases—are typically in place to make these decisions.

2

Identify the biases most likely to affect critical decisions

Open discussion of the biases that may be undermining decision making is invaluable. It can be stimulated both by conducting postmortems of past decisions and by observing current decision processes. Are we at risk, in this meeting, of being too action oriented? Do I see someone who thinks he recognizes a pattern but whose choice of analogies seems misleading to me? Are we seeing biases combine to create dysfunctional patterns that, when repeated in an organization, can become cultural traits? For example, is the combination of social and status quo biases creating a culture of consensus-based inertia? This discussion will help surface the biases to which the decision process under review is particularly prone.

3

Select practices and tools to counter the most relevant biases

Companies should select mechanisms that are appropriate to the type of decision at hand, to their culture, and to the decision-making styles of their leaders. For instance, one company we know counters social biases by organizing, as part of its annual planning cycle, a systematic challenge by outsiders to its business units' plans. Another fights pattern-recognition biases by asking managers who present a recommendation to share the raw data supporting it, so other executives in this analytically minded company can try to discern alternative patterns.

If, as you read these lines, you have already thought of three reasons these techniques won't work in your own company's culture, you are probably right. The question is which ones *will*. Adopting behavioral strategy means not only embracing the broad principles set forth above but also selecting and tailoring specific debiasing practices to turn the principles into action.

4

Embed practices in formal processes

By embedding these practices in formal corporate operating procedures (such as capital-investment approval processes or R&D reviews), executives can ensure that such techniques are used with some regularity and not just when the ultimate decision maker feels unusually uncertain about which call to make. One reason it's important to embed these practices in recurring procedures is that everything we know about the tendency toward overconfidence suggests that it is unwise to rely on one's instincts to decide when to rely on one's instincts! Another is that good decision making requires practice as a management team: without regular opportunities, the team will agree in principle on the techniques it should use but lack the experience (and the mutual trust) to use them effectively.

• • •

The behavioral-strategy journey requires effort and the commitment of senior leadership, but the payoff—better decisions, not to mention more engaged managers—makes it one of the most valuable strategic investments organizations can make. o

A language to discuss biases

Psychologists and behavioral economists have identified dozens of cognitive biases. The typology we present here is not meant to be exhaustive but rather to focus on those biases that occur most frequently and that have the largest impact on business decisions. As these groupings make clear, one of the insidious things about cognitive biases is their close relationship with the rules of thumb and mind-sets that often serve managers well. For example, many a seasoned executive rightly prides herself on pattern-recognition skills cultivated over the years. Similarly, seeking consensus when making a decision is often not a failing but a condition of success. And valuing stability rather than "rocking the boat" or "fixing what ain't broke" is a sound management precept.

This bias typology was prepared by Dan Lovallo and Olivier Sibony.

Action-oriented biases
drive us to take action less thoughtfully than we should.

Excessive optimism. The tendency for people to be overoptimistic about the outcome of planned actions, to overestimate the likelihood of positive events, and to underestimate the likelihood of negative ones.

Overconfidence. Overestimating our skill level relative to others', leading us to overestimate our ability to affect future outcomes, take credit for past outcomes, and neglect the role of chance.

Competitor neglect. The tendency to plan without factoring in competitive responses, as if one is playing tennis against a wall, not a live opponent.

Interest biases
arise in the presence of conflicting incentives, including nonmonetary and even purely emotional ones.

Misaligned individual incentives. Incentives for individuals in organizations to adopt views or to seek outcomes favorable to their unit or themselves, at the expense of the overall interest of the company. These self-serving views are often held genuinely, not cynically.

Inappropriate attachments. Emotional attachment of individuals to people or elements of the business (such as legacy products or brands), creating a misalignment of interests.[1]

Misaligned perception of corporate goals. Disagreements (often unspoken) about the hierarchy or relative weight of objectives pursued by the organization and about the trade-offs between them.

[1] Sydney Finkelstein, Jo Whitehead, and Andrew Campbell, *Think Again: Why Good Leaders Make Bad Decisions and How to Keep It from Happening to You,* Boston: Harvard Business Press, 2008.

Pattern-recognition biases

lead us to recognize patterns even where there are none.

Confirmation bias. The over-weighting of evidence consistent with a favored belief, underweighting of evidence against a favored belief, or failure to search impartially for evidence.

Management by example. Generalizing based on examples that are particularly recent or memorable.

False analogies—especially, misleading experiences. Relying on comparisons with situations that are not directly comparable.

Power of storytelling. The tendency to remember and to believe more easily a set of facts when they are presented as part of a coherent story.

Champion bias. The tendency to evaluate a plan or proposal based on the track record of the person presenting it, more than on the facts supporting it.

Stability biases

create a tendency toward inertia in the presence of uncertainty.

Anchoring and insufficient adjustment. Rooting oneself to an initial value, leading to insufficient adjustments of subsequent estimates.

Loss aversion. The tendency to feel losses more acutely than gains of the same amount, making us more risk-averse than a rational calculation would suggest.

Sunk-cost fallacy. Paying attention to historical costs that are not recoverable when considering future courses of action.

Status quo bias. Preference for the status quo in the absence of pressure to change it.

Social biases

arise from the preference for harmony over conflict.

Groupthink. Striving for consensus at the cost of a realistic appraisal of alternative courses of action.

Sunflower management. Tendency for groups to align with the views of their leaders, whether expressed or assumed.

To listen to the authors narrate a more comprehensive presentation of these biases and the ways they can combine to create dysfunctional patterns in corporate cultures, visit mckinseyquarterly.com.

How we do it:
Three executives reflect on
strategic decision making

**WPP's Sir
Martin Sorrell**

**Kleiner Perkins'
Randy Komisar**

**Xerox's
Anne Mulcahy**

'Learn from mistakes and listen to feedback,

Sir Martin Sorrell

Sir Martin Sorrell is chief executive officer of WPP, a leading advertising and marketing-services group. Sir Martin actively supports the advancement of international business schools, advising Harvard, IESE, the London Business School, and Indian School of Business, among others.

The reality is that leaders must, on the spur of the moment, be able to react rapidly and grasp opportunities. Ultimately, therefore, I think that the best process to reduce the risk of bad decisions—whatever series of tests, hurdles, and measuring sticks one applies—should be quick, flexible, and largely informal. It's important to experiment, to be open to intuition, and to listen to flashes of inspiration. This is not to say the process shouldn't be rigorous: run the analyses, suck up all the data, and include some formal processes as well. But don't ask hundreds of people. Carefully sound out the relevant constituencies—clients, suppliers, competitors—and try to find someone you trust who has no agenda about the issue at hand.

There will be mistakes, of course. The truth is we all make mistakes all the time. For instance, I know it's true that decision makers risk escalating their commitment to losing endeavors that they have an emotional stake in. I know because I've been guilty of that myself. However, the only way to avoid making mistakes is to avoid making decisions (or, at least, very few). But then the company would grind to a halt. Instead, learn from mistakes and listen to feedback. o

'Balance out biases'

Randy Komisar

Before behavioral economics even had a name, it shook up Randy Komisar's career. He became aware of the then-nascent field while contemplating a graduate degree in economics, losing confidence in the dismal science as a result. Komisar ultimately shifted gears, becoming a lawyer and later pursuing a career in commerce. He cofounded Claris,[1] served as CEO for LucasArts Entertainment and Crystal Dynamics, served as "virtual CEO" for a host of companies such as WebTV[2] and TiVo and, since 2005, has been a partner at Kleiner Perkins Caufield & Byers, the Silicon Valley venture capital fund. Along the way, he has developed a distinct point of view on how to create executive teams and cultural environments that are conducive to good decision making. In a recent interview with McKinsey's Olivier Sibony and Allen Webb, Komisar provided practical advice for senior executives hoping to make good decisions in a world where bias is inevitable.

[1] Claris is now FileMaker.
[2] WebTV is now MSN TV.

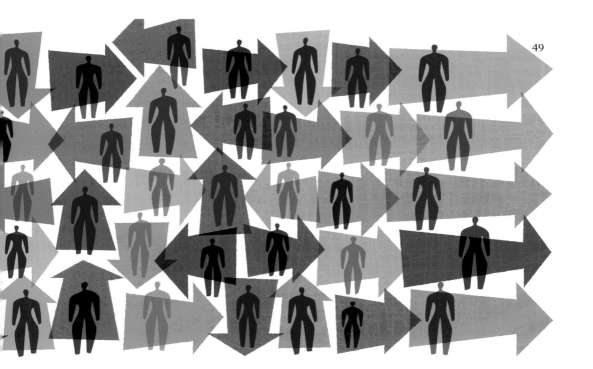

49

Randy Komisar is a partner with Kleiner Perkins Caufield & Byers. He is the author of *The Monk and the Riddle* and coauthor, with John Mullins, of *Getting to Plan B: Breaking Through to a* *Better Business Model.* Randy has been a consulting professor of entrepreneurship at Stanford, where he still lectures.

Harness bias

Rather than trying to tune out bias, my focus is on recognizing, encouraging, and balancing bias within effective decision making. I came to that conclusion as I was starting my career, when I had a chance to work with Bill Campbell, who is well known, particularly in Silicon Valley, as a leader and coach. Bill was the CEO of Intuit (where he's now chairman), he's on the Apple board, and he's a consigliore to Google.[3]

What I observed back then was that Bill had this amazing ability to bring together a ragtag team of exceptionally talented people. Some had worked for successful companies, some had not. Some had been senior managers. Some had been individual contributors. Everybody brought to the table biases borne out of their domains and their experiences. Those experience-based biases probably are not that

[3] For more on Bill Campbell, see Lenny Mendonca and Kevin D. Sneader, "Coaching innovation: An interview with Intuit's Bill Campbell," mckinseyquarterly.com, February 2007.

different at the psychological level from the behavioral biases that economists focus on today.

Bill was very capable at balancing out the biases around the table and coming up with really effective decisions and, more important, the groundwork for consensus—not necessarily unanimity, but consensus. I liken it to what I have always understood, true or false, about how President Kennedy ran his cabinet: that he used to assemble the smartest people he could, throw a difficult issue on the table, and watch them debate it. Then at some point he would end the debate, make a decision, and move on. It's also similar to the judicial process, where advocates come together to present every facet of a case, and a judge makes an informed determination. The advocates' biases actually work to the benefit of a good decision, rather than being something that needs to be mitigated.

Make a balance sheet

There's a methodology I've used within companies for making big, hard decisions that I introduced into Kleiner Perkins and that we have been using lately to help decide whether or not to invest in new ventures. It starts with assembling a group that is very diverse. If you look at my partners, you'd see an unruly gang of talented people with very different experiences, very different domain skills, and, consequently, very different opinions.

Starting with that, the notion is to put together a simple balance sheet where everybody around the table is asked to list points on both sides: "Tell me what is good about this opportunity; tell me what is bad about it. Do not tell me your judgment yet. I don't want to know." They start the process without having to justify and thereby freeze their opinions and instead are allowed to give their best insights and consider the ideas of others. Not surprisingly, smart people will uncover many of the same issues. But they may weigh them differently depending on their biases.

We do not ask for anyone's bottom line until everybody has spoken and the full balance sheet is revealed. I have noticed my own judgment often changes as I see the balance sheet fill out. I might have said, "We shouldn't do the deal for the following three reasons." But after creating a balance sheet, I might well look at it and say, "You know, it's probably worth doing for these two reasons."

The balance sheet process mitigates a lot of the friction that typically arises when people marshal the facts that support their case while ignoring those that don't. It also emphasizes to the group that each participant is smart and knowledgeable, that it was a difficult

The balance sheet process allows everyone around the table to give their best insights and consider the ideas of others, without having to justify and thereby freeze their opinions

decision, and that there is ample room for the other judgment. By assembling everyone's insights rather than their conclusions, the discussion can focus on the biases and assumptions that lead to the opinions. An added bonus is that people start to see their own biases. Somebody will stand up and say, "You're expecting me to say the following three things, and I will. But I've also got to tell you about these other four things, which are probably not what you'd expect from me." Finally, opinion leaders have less sway because they don't signal their conclusions too early.

Although this may sound tedious and slow, we're able to move quickly. One reason is that we never try to achieve perfection—meaning 100 percent certainty—around a decision. We just can't get there in the timeframe necessary. The corollary is that we assume every decision needs to be tested, measured, and refined. If the test results come back positive, we proceed; if they're negative, we "course correct" quickly.

Create a culture where 'failure' is not a wrong answer

The book John Mullins and I recently wrote, *Getting to Plan B*, presents a way of building a culture of good decision making.[4] The very simple premise is that Plan *A* most often fails, so we need a process by which to methodically test assumptions to get to a better Plan *B*.

The process starts with an acknowledgment that Plan *A* probably is based upon flawed assumptions, and that certain leap-of-faith questions are fundamental to arriving at a better answer. If we disagree on the decision, it's very likely that we have different assumptions on those

---

[4] *Getting to Plan B: Breaking Through to a Better Business Model,* Watertown, MA: Harvard Business Press, 2009.

critical questions—and we need to decide which assumptions are stronger, yours or mine. You end up teasing apart these assumptions through analogs: someone will say, "Joe did something like this." And then someone else will say, "Yes, but Joe's situation was different for the following reasons. Sally did something like this, and it failed." In that process, you don't get points for being right about your assumption, and I don't lose points for being wrong. We both get points for identifying the assumption, working on it, and agreeing that the facts have come in one way or the other.

What makes this culturally difficult in larger companies is that there is often a sense that Plan *A* is going to succeed. It's well analyzed. It's vetted. It's crisp. It looks great on an Excel spreadsheet. It becomes the plan of record to which everybody executes. And the execution of that plan does not usually contemplate testing assumptions on an ongoing basis to permit a course correction. So if the plan is wrong, which it most often is, then it is a total failure. The work has gone on too long. Too much money has been spent. Too many people have invested their time and attention on it. And careers can be hurt in the process. To create the right culture, you have to make very clear that a wrong answer is not "failure" unless it is ignored or uncorrectable.

Intuit, for instance, has found that many early-stage R&D projects went on too long. As in most companies, there was a belief that "we just need to put a little more time and money into these things." Within about 90 days after I had explained the Plan *B* process to Intuit, they had broken a set of projects into smaller hypotheses, put together a dashboard process for testing assumptions, and were starting to make go-no-go decisions at each step along the way. They reported back that teams were killing their own projects early because they now had metrics to guide them. And most important, they were not being blamed. Intuit's culture allows for rapid testing and "failure," and those who prove responsible and accountable in course correcting are rewarded with new projects.

Listen to the little voice

I think comfort with uncertainty and ambiguity is an important trait in a leader. That's not to say that they're ambiguous or uncertain or unclear, but they're not hiding behind some notion of black or white. When somebody's shutting down conversations because he is uncomfortable with the points of view in the room or with where the decision may be going, it usually leads to a culture where the best ideas no longer come to the top.

Now, there are cultures where that does seem to work, but I think those are exceptions. Steve Jobs seems to be able to run Apple exceedingly well in large part because Steve Jobs is an extraordinary person. But he's not a guy who tolerates a lot of diversity of opinion. Frankly, few leaders I meet, no matter how important they are in the press or how big their paychecks are, are that comfortable with diversity of opinion.

I love a leader who changes his or her opinion based upon the strength of the arguments around the table. It's great to see a leader concede that the decision's a hard one and may have to be retested. It's great to see a leader who will echo the little voice in the back of the room that has a different point of view—and thereby change the complexion of the discussion.

When I went to LucasArts, I can remember sitting down one day with a young woman two levels down in the sales organization. I said, "Do you think we could build our own sales force and distribution here? We've been going through distributors for a long time. Our margins are a lot smaller as a result. What do you think?" She shut the door, looked at me, and said, "I know that my boss would disagree with me and I know that my peers in marketing disagree with me, but I think we can do it." And so we did it, and the company's gross margin line probably grew fivefold in 12 months—all based upon this one little voice in the back of the room. You've got to be able to hear that voice. o

❝Timeliness trumps perfection❞

Anne Mulcahy

Anne Mulcahy is chairman and former CEO of Xerox. She is a director on the boards of Catalyst, Citigroup, Johnson & Johnson, and the Washington Post Company, as well as chair of the board of trustees for Save the Children.

When Anne Mulcahy became CEO of Xerox in 2001—as the company teetered on the edge of bankruptcy—she dove in with the confidence and decisiveness that had typified her career to date. But as she began to engineer the company's dramatic turnaround, something unexpected happened: Mulcahy started hearing rumblings that her leadership style was too decisive. As she recounts, "I got feedback that between my directness and my body language, within three nanoseconds people knew where I stood on everything and lined up to follow, and that if I didn't work on it, it really would be a problem." So Mulcahy listened. "I stopped getting on my feet," she explains, "and I worked hard at not jumping in, at making people express a point of view."

This was the first of many lessons about how to ensure high-quality decision making that Mulcahy would go on to learn during her nine years as CEO. In a recent interview with McKinsey's Rik Kirkland, she distilled five suggestions for other senior leaders.

Cultivate internal critics

My own management style probably hasn't changed much in 20 years, but I learned to compensate for this by building a team that could counter some of my own weaknesses. You need internal critics: people who know what impact you're having and who have the courage to give you that feedback. I learned how to groom those critics early on, and that was really, really useful. This requires a certain comfort with confrontation, though, so it's a skill that has to be developed.

I started making a point of saying, "All right, John-Noel, what are you thinking? I need to hear." And this started to demonstrate that even if I did show my colors quickly, they could still take me on and I could still change my mind. The decisions that come out of allowing people to have different views—and treasuring the diversity of those views—are often harder to implement than what comes out of consensus decision making, but they're also better.

Force tough people choices

If you're sitting around the table with the wrong group of people, no process is going to drive good decision making. You need to lead with people decisions first. One of the easiest mistakes you can make is to compromise on people. It's very easy to close your eyes and say warm bodies are better than no bodies. The way to counter this bias is to introduce a "forced choice" process. What I mean by this is, you need a disciplined process for forcing discussion about a set of candidates and a position. At Xerox, we developed an HR process that required three candidates for every job.

We also established a group-assessment process, which helped us avoid what I call lazy people decisions, that is, biases against confrontation that could have marginalized the effectiveness of our team. You need to look for people who can strike the hard balance between courage and learning—people who have audacity in their convictions and know when to be unyielding but who are also good listeners and capable of adapting. That is the single most important leadership trait, outside of pure competence.

However you do it, you need to set a context for choice. Once you've done that, you must make sure you understand your own criteria for what first-class talent means, and you need to hold yourself accountable for creating a dialogue about it in a very honest way.

Force tough R&D choices

One of the rules of the road should be never to evaluate R&D programs individually. You should always decide on them within the context of an R&D portfolio. There needs to be an "is this better than that?" conversation—no one should get to personally champion his program in a vacuum. Any single idea can look great in isolation.

The portfolio process, like the "forced choice" process for people decisions, is really important because it gives you choices in context. It also takes some of the difficulty of killing individual projects out of the way. And it helps you hold yourself accountable for the full resourcing of the idea. If you decide to invest in a growth opportunity, it's because you've spent a lot of time making sure that it's resourced properly, that you've got the right skill sets to execute it, and that you're not just saying, "Sure, go off and do it" before you've thought through all those considerations.

This process was particularly important for us at Xerox. We kept an investment going for ten years in a technology called Solid Ink, which just came to market this year. We did this by putting a fence around it and a few other strategic priorities that we knew we wanted to protect. Portfolio decision making helped us drive those priorities forward even though most of the people who made the decisions wouldn't still be in their jobs to see the returns.

Know when to let go

One of the most important types of decision making is deciding what you are *not* going to do, what you need to eliminate in order to make room for strategic investments. This could mean shutting down a program. It could mean outsourcing part of the business. These are often the hardest decisions to make, and the ones that don't get nearly enough focus. Making a decision not to fund a new project is not painful. Making a decision to take out a historical program or investment is. It means taking out people and competencies and expertise. That's much, much harder.

The most difficult decisions are these legacy ones—the historical investments, the things that are just easier to chip away at rather than make a tough decision. This is where we make the most compromises— at the expense of our focus. A great example from Xerox was that it took too long to move from legacy investments in black-and-white imaging to future strategic investments in color and services.

An approach that can help this process involves establishing a decision framework (one akin to a zero-based budgeting philosophy) that says there's no preconceived commitment to a legacy business. It will get discussed in the context of opportunities for future investment like all the rest. But to make this decision process work, you need to make sure to create a balance between the people who can champion and advocate the future and those who own—and are very invested in—the past.

Strike the right risk balance

Decisiveness is about timeliness. And timeliness trumps perfection. The most damaging decisions are the missed opportunities, the decisions that didn't get made in time. If you're creating a category of bad decisions you've made, you need to include with it all the decisions you *didn't* get to make because you missed the window of time that existed to take advantage of an opportunity.

These days, everyone is risk averse. Unfortunately, people define risk as something you avoid rather than something you take. But taking risks is critical to your decision-making effectiveness and growth, and most companies have taken a large step backwards because of the current climate. I was CEO of Xerox for five years before we really got back into the acquisition market, even though we knew we needed to acquire some things rather than develop them internally. But we got very conservative, very risk averse, and also too data driven. By the time we would reach a decision that some technology was going to be a home run, it had either already been bought or was so expensive we couldn't afford it.

Decisions have shelf lives, so you really need to put tight timeframes on your process. I would so much rather live with the outcome of making a few bad decisions than miss a boatload of good ones. Some of it flies in the face of good process and just requires good gut. So when trying to take bias out of decision making, you need to be really cautious not to take instinct, courage, and gut out as well.○

When can you trust your gut?

Nobel laureate Daniel Kahneman and psychologist Gary Klein debate the power and perils of intuition for senior executives.

For two scholars representing opposing schools of thought, Daniel Kahneman and Gary Klein find a surprising amount of common ground. Kahneman, a psychologist, won the Nobel Prize in economics in 2002 for prospect theory, which helps explain the sometimes counter-intuitive choices people make under uncertainty. Klein, a senior scientist at MacroCognition, has focused on the power of intuition to support good decision making in high-pressure environments, such as firefighting and intensive-care units.

In a September 2009 *American Psychology* article titled "Conditions for intuitive expertise: A failure to disagree," Kahneman and Klein debated the circumstances in which intuition would yield good decision making. In this interview with Olivier Sibony, a director in McKinsey's Brussels office, and Dan Lovallo, a professor at the University of Sydney and an adviser to McKinsey, Kahneman and Klein explore the power and perils of intuition for senior executives.

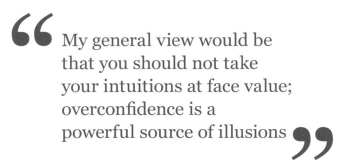

My general view would be
that you should not take
your intuitions at face value;
overconfidence is a
powerful source of illusions

Daniel Kahneman is a Nobel laureate
and a professor emeritus of psychology and public
affairs at Princeton University's Woodrow Wilson
School. He is also a fellow at the Hebrew University
of Jerusalem and a Gallup senior scientist.

The *Quarterly*: *In your recent* American Psychology *article, you asked a question that should be interesting to just about all executives: "Under what conditions are the intuitions of professionals worthy of trust?" What's your answer? When can executives trust their guts?*

Gary Klein: It depends on what you mean by "trust." If you mean, "My gut feeling is telling me this; therefore I can act on it and I don't have to worry," we say you should never trust your gut. You need to take your gut feeling as an important data point, but then you have to consciously and deliberately evaluate it, to see if it makes sense in this context. You need strategies that help rule things out. That's the opposite of saying, "This is what my gut is telling me; let me gather information to confirm it."

Daniel Kahneman: There are some conditions where you have to trust your intuition. When you are under time pressure for a decision, you need to follow intuition. My general view, though, would be that you should not take your intuitions at face value. Overconfidence is a powerful source of illusions, primarily determined by the quality and coherence of the story that you can construct, not by its validity. If people can construct a simple and coherent story, they will feel confident regardless of how well grounded it is in reality.

The *Quarterly*: *Is intuition more reliable under certain conditions?*

Gary Klein: We identified two. First, there needs to be a certain structure to a situation, a certain predictability that allows you to have a basis for the intuition. If a situation is very, very turbulent, we say it has low validity, and there's no basis for intuition. For example, you shouldn't trust the judgments of stock brokers picking individual stocks. The second factor is whether decision makers have a chance to get feedback on their judgments, so that they can strengthen them and gain expertise. If those criteria aren't met, then intuitions aren't going to be trustworthy.

Most corporate decisions aren't going to meet the test of high validity. But they're going to be way above the low-validity situations that we worry about. Many business intuitions and expertise are going to be valuable; they are telling you something useful, and you want to take advantage of them.

Daniel Kahneman: This is an area of difference between Gary and me. I would be wary of experts' intuition, except when they deal with something that they have dealt with a lot in the past. Surgeons, for example, do many operations of a given kind, and they learn what

Many business intuitions and expertise are going to be valuable; they are telling you something useful, and you want to take advantage of them

Gary Klein is a cognitive psychologist and senior scientist at MacroCognition. He is the author of *Sources of Power: How People Make Decisions*, *The Power of Intuition*, and *Streetlights and Shadows: Searching for the Keys to Adaptive Decision Making*.

problems they're going to encounter. But when problems are unique, or fairly unique, then I would be less trusting of intuition than Gary is. One of the problems with expertise is that people have it in some domains and not in others. So experts don't know exactly where the boundaries of their expertise are.

The *Quarterly*: *Many executives would argue that major strategic decisions, such as market entry, M&A, or R&D investments, take place in environments where their experience counts—what you might call high-validity environments. Are they right?*

Gary Klein: None of those really involve high-validity environments, but there's enough structure for executives to listen to their intuitions. I'd like to see a mental simulation that involves looking at ways each of the options could play out or imagining ways that they could go sour, as well as discovering why people are excited about them.

Daniel Kahneman: In strategic decisions, I'd be really concerned about overconfidence. There are often entire aspects of the problem that you can't see—for example, am I ignoring what competitors might do? An executive might have a very strong intuition that a given product has promise, without considering the probability that a rival is already ahead in developing the same product. I'd add that the amount of success it takes for leaders to become overconfident isn't terribly large. Some achieve a reputation for great successes when in fact all they have done is take chances that reasonable people wouldn't take.

Gary Klein: Danny and I are in agreement that by the time executives get to high levels, they are good at making others feel confident in their judgment, even if there's no strong basis for the judgment.

The *Quarterly*: *So you would argue that selection processes for leaders tend to favor lucky risk takers rather than the wise?*

Daniel Kahneman: No question—if there's a bias, it's in that direction. Beyond that, lucky risk takers use hindsight to reinforce their feeling that their gut is very wise. Hindsight also reinforces others' trust in that individual's gut. That's one of the real dangers of leader selection in many organizations: leaders are selected for overconfidence. We associate leadership with decisiveness. That perception of leadership pushes people to make decisions fairly quickly, lest they be seen as dithering and indecisive.

Gary Klein: I agree. Society's epitome of credibility is John Wayne, who sizes up a situation and says, "Here's what I'm going to do"— and you follow him. We both worry about leaders in complex situations

Overconfidence in action?

Does management admit mistakes and kill unsuccessful initiatives in a timely manner?

C-level execs

Yes **80%**

No **20%**

Non-C-level

Yes **49%**

No **52%**

Source: December 2009 survey of 463 executive readers of the *McKinsey Quarterly*

 Executives responded to the survey after reading "Competing through organizational agility," by London Business School professor Don Sull, on mckinseyquarterly.com.

who don't have enough experience, who are just going with their intuition and not monitoring it, not thinking about it.

Daniel Kahneman: There's a cost to *not* being John Wayne, since there really is a strong expectation that leaders will be decisive and act quickly. We deeply want to be led by people who know what they're doing and who don't have to think about it too much.

The *Quarterly*: *Who would be your poster child for the "non–John Wayne" type of leader?*

Gary Klein: I met a lieutenant general in Iraq who told me a marvelous story about his first year there. He kept learning things he didn't know. He did that by continuously challenging his assumptions when he realized he was wrong. At the end of the year, he had a completely different view of how to do things, and he didn't lose credibility. Another example I would offer is Lou Gerstner when he went to IBM. He entered an industry that he didn't understand. He didn't pretend to understand the nuances, but he was seen as intelligent and open minded, and he gained trust very quickly.

The *Quarterly*: *A moment ago, Gary, you talked about imagining ways a decision could go sour. That sounds reminiscent of your "premortem" technique. Could you please say a little more about that?*

Gary Klein: The premortem technique is a sneaky way to get people to do contrarian, devil's advocate thinking without encountering resistance. If a project goes poorly, there will be a lessons-learned session that looks at what went wrong and why the project failed—like a medical postmortem. Why don't we do that up front? Before a project starts, we should say, "We're looking in a crystal ball, and this project has failed; it's a fiasco. Now, everybody, take two minutes and write down all the reasons why you think the project failed."

The logic is that instead of showing people that you are smart because you can come up with a good plan, you show you're smart by thinking of insightful reasons why this project might go south. If you make it part of your corporate culture, then you create an interesting competition: "I want to come up with some possible problem that other people haven't even thought of." The whole dynamic changes from trying to avoid anything that might disrupt harmony to trying to surface potential problems.

Daniel Kahneman: The premortem is a great idea. I mentioned it at Davos—giving full credit to Gary—and the chairman of a large corporation said it was worth coming to Davos for. The beauty of the premortem is that it is very easy to do. My guess is that, in general, doing a premortem on a plan that is about to be adopted won't cause it to be abandoned. But it will probably be tweaked in ways that everybody will recognize as beneficial. So the premortem is a low-cost, high-payoff kind of thing.

The *Quarterly*: *It sounds like you agree on the benefits of the premortem and in your thinking about leadership. Where don't you see eye to eye?*

Daniel Kahneman: I like checklists as a solution; Gary doesn't.

Gary Klein: I'm not an opponent of checklists for high-validity environments with repetitive tasks. I don't want my pilot forgetting to fill out the pretakeoff checklist! But I'm less enthusiastic about checklists when you move into environments that are more complex and ambiguous, because that's where you need expertise. Checklists are about if/then statements. The checklist tells you the "then" but you need expertise to determine the "if"—has the condition been satisfied? In a dynamic, ambiguous environment, this requires judgment, and it's hard to put that into checklists.

Daniel Kahneman: I disagree. In situations where you don't have high validity, that's where you need checklists the most. The checklist doesn't guarantee that you won't make errors when the situation is uncertain. But it may prevent you from being overconfident. I view that as a good thing.

The problem is that people don't really like checklists; there's resistance to them. So you have to turn them into a standard operating procedure—for example, at the stage of due diligence, when board members go through a checklist before they approve a decision. A checklist like that would be about process, not content. I don't think you can have checklists and quality control all over the place, but in a few strategic environments, I think they are worth trying.

The _Quarterly_: _What should be on a checklist when an executive is making an important strategic decision?_

Daniel Kahneman: I would ask about the quality and independence of information. Is it coming from multiple sources or just one source that's being regurgitated in different ways? Is there a possibility of group-think? Does the leader have an opinion that seems to be influencing others? I would ask where every number comes from and would try to postpone the achievement of group consensus. Fragmenting problems and keeping judgments independent helps decorrelate errors of judgment.

The _Quarterly_: _Could you explain what you mean by "correlated errors"?_

Daniel Kahneman: Sure. There's a classic experiment where you ask people to estimate how many coins there are in a transparent jar. When people do that independently, the accuracy of the judgment rises with the number of estimates, when they are averaged. But if people hear each other make estimates, the first one influences the second, which influences the third, and so on. That's what I call a correlated error.

Frankly, I'm surprised that when you have a reasonably well-informed group—say, they have read all the background materials—that it isn't more common to begin by having everyone write their conclusions on a slip of paper. If you don't do that, the discussion will create an enormous amount of conformity that reduces the quality of the judgment.

The _Quarterly_: _Beyond checklists, do you disagree in other important ways?_

Gary Klein: Danny and I aren't lined up on whether there's more to be gained by listening to intuitions or by stifling them until you have a chance to get all the information. Performance depends on having important insights as well as avoiding errors. But sometimes, I believe, the techniques you use to reduce the chance of error can get in the way of gaining insights.

Daniel Kahneman: My advice would be to try to postpone intuition as much as possible. Take the example of an acquisition. Ultimately, you are going to end up with a number—what the target company will cost you. If you get to specific numbers too early, you will anchor on those numbers, and they'll get much more weight than they actually deserve. You do as much homework as possible beforehand so that the intuition is as informed as it can be.

The *Quarterly*: *What is the best point in the decision process for an intervention that aims to eliminate bias?*

Daniel Kahneman: It's when you decide what information needs to be collected. That's an absolutely critical step. If you're starting with a hypothesis and planning to collect information, make sure that the process is systematic and the information high quality. This should take place fairly early.

Gary Klein: I don't think executives are saying, "I have my hypothesis and I'm looking only for data that will support it." I think the process is rather that people make quick judgments about what's happening, which allows them to determine what information is relevant. Otherwise, they get into an information overload mode. Rather than seeking confirmation, they're using the frames that come from their experience to guide their search. Of course, it's easy for people to lose track of how much they've explained away. So one possibility is to try to surface this for them—to show them the list of things that they've explained away.

Daniel Kahneman: I'd add that hypothesis testing can be completely contaminated if the organization knows the answer that the leader wants to get. You want to create the possibility that people can discover that an idea is a lousy one early in the game, before the whole machinery is committed to it.

The *Quarterly*: *How optimistic are you that individuals can debias themselves?*

Daniel Kahneman: I'm really not optimistic. Most decision makers will trust their own intuitions because they think they see the situation clearly. It's a special exercise to question your own intuitions.

I think that almost the only way to learn how to debias yourself is to learn to critique other people. I call that "educating gossip." If we could elevate the gossip about decision making by introducing terms such as "anchoring," from the study of errors, into the language of organizations, people could talk about other people's mistakes in a more refined way.

The *Quarterly*: *Do you think corporate leaders want to generate that type of gossip? How do they typically react to your ideas?*

Daniel Kahneman: The reaction is always the same—they are very interested, but unless they invited you specifically because they wanted to do something, they don't want to apply anything. Except for the premortem. People just love the premortem.

The *Quarterly*: *Why do you think leaders are hesitant to act on your ideas?*

Daniel Kahneman: That's easy. Leaders know that any procedure they put in place is going to cause their judgment to be questioned. And whether they're fully aware of it or not, they're really not in the market to have their decisions and choices questioned.

The *Quarterly*: *Yet senior executives want to make good decisions. Do you have any final words of wisdom for them in that quest?*

Daniel Kahneman: My single piece of advice would be to improve the quality of meetings—that seems pretty strategic to improving the quality of decision making. People spend a lot of time in meetings. You want meetings to be short. People should have a lot of information, and you want to decorrelate errors.

Gary Klein: What concerns me is the tendency to marginalize people who disagree with you at meetings. There's too much intolerance for challenge. As a leader, you can say the right things—for instance, everybody should share their opinions. But people are too smart to do that, because it's risky. So when people raise an idea that doesn't make sense to you as a leader, rather than ask what's wrong with them, you should be curious about why they're taking the position. Curiosity is a counterforce for contempt when people are making unpopular statements. o

Taking the bias out of meetings

These meeting guidelines were prepared by Dan Lovallo and Olivier Sibony.

The biases that undermine strategic decision making often operate in meetings. Here is a menu of ideas for running them in a way that will mitigate the impact of those biases. Not every suggestion will be applicable to all types of decisions or organizations, but paying attention to the principles underlying these ideas should pay dividends for any executive trying to run meetings that lead to sounder decisions.

Make sure the right people are involved

Ensure diversity of backgrounds, roles, risk aversion profiles, and interests; cultivate critics within the top team (for more on cultivating critics, see p. 55).

Invite contributions based on expertise, not rank. Don't hesitate to invite expert contributors to come and present a point of view without attending the entire meeting.

For the portion of the meeting where a decision is going to be made, keep attendance to a minimum, preferably with a team that has experience making decisions together. This loads the dice in favor of depersonalized debate by eliminating executives' fear of exposing their subordinates to conflict and also creates, over time, an environment of trust among that small group of decision makers.

Assign homework

Make sure predecision due diligence is based on accurate, sufficient, and independent facts and on appropriate analytical techniques.

Request alternatives and "out of the box" plans—for instance, by soliciting input from outsiders to the decision-making process.

Consider setting up competing fact-gathering teams charged with investigating opposing hypotheses.

Create the right atmosphere

As the final decision maker, ask others to speak up (starting with the most junior person); show you can change your mind based on their input; strive to create a "peerlike" atmosphere.

Encourage admissions of individual experiences and interests that create possible biases (for more on the role of past experiences, see pp. 37–38).

Encourage expressions of doubt and create a climate that recognizes reasonable people may disagree when discussing difficult decisions.

Encourage substantive disagreements on the issue at hand by clearly dissociating it from personal conflict, using humor to defuse tension.

Manage the debate

Before you get going, make sure everyone knows the meeting's purpose (making a decision) and the criteria you will be using to make that decision. For recurring decisions (such as R&D portfolio reviews), make it clear to everyone that those criteria include "forcing devices" (such as comparing projects against one another).

Take the pulse of the room: ask participants to write down their initial positions, use voting devices, or ask participants for their "balance sheets" of pros and cons (for more on balance sheets, see pp. 50–51).

Use the premortem technique to expand the debate (for more on the premortem, see p. 64).

Counter anchoring: postpone the introduction of numbers if possible; "reframe" alternative courses of action as they emerge, by making explicit "what you have to believe" to support each of the alternatives (for more on postponing numbers and making assumptions explicit, see pp. 51–52 and 65–66).

Pay attention to the use of comparisons and analogies: limit the use of inappropriate ones ("inadmissible evidence") by asking for alternatives and suggesting or requesting additional analogies.

Force the room to consider opposing views. For vital decisions, create an explicit role for one or two people—the "decision challengers."

Follow up

Commit yourself to the decision. Debate should stop when the decision is made. Connect individually with initial dissenters and make sure implementation plans address their concerns to the extent possible.

Monitor pre–agreed upon criteria and milestones to correct your course or move on to backup plans.

Conduct a postmortem on the decision once its outcome is known.

Periodically step back and review decision processes to improve meeting preparation and mechanics, using an outside observer to diagnose possible sources of bias.

 To listen to a podcast in which the authors discuss additional insights on taking the bias out of meetings, visit mckinseyquarterly.com.

The Internet of Things

**Michael Chui,
Markus Löffler, and
Roger Roberts**

More objects are becoming embedded with sensors and gaining the ability to communicate. The resulting information networks promise to create new business models, improve business processes, and reduce costs and risks.

In most organizations, information travels along familiar routes. Proprietary information is lodged in databases and analyzed in reports and then rises up the management chain. Information also originates externally—gathered from public sources, harvested from the Internet, or purchased from information suppliers.

But the predictable pathways of information are changing: the physical world itself is becoming a type of information system. In what's called the Internet of Things, sensors and actuators embedded in physical objects—from roadways to pacemakers—are linked through wired and wireless networks, often using the same Internet Protocol (IP) that connects the Internet. These networks churn out huge volumes of data that flow to computers for analysis. When objects can both sense the environment and communicate, they become tools for understanding complexity and responding to it swiftly. What's revolutionary in all this is that these physical information systems are now beginning to be deployed, and some of them even work largely without human intervention.

Michael Chui is a
senior fellow with
the McKinsey Global
Institute, Markus
Löffler is a principal in
McKinsey's Stuttgart
office, and Roger
Roberts is a principal
in the Silicon Valley
office.

Pill-shaped microcameras already traverse the human digestive tract and send back thousands of images to pinpoint sources of illness. Precision farming equipment with wireless links to data collected from remote satellites and ground sensors can take into account crop conditions and adjust the way each individual part of a field is farmed—

for instance, by spreading extra fertilizer on areas that need more nutrients. Billboards in Japan peer back at passersby, assessing how they fit consumer profiles, and instantly change displayed messages based on those assessments.

Yes, there are traces of futurism in some of this and early warnings for companies too. Business models based on today's largely static information architectures face challenges as new ways of creating value arise. When a customer's buying preferences are sensed in real time at a specific location, dynamic pricing may increase the odds of a purchase. Knowing how often or intensively a product is used can create additional options—usage fees rather than outright sale, for example. Manufacturing processes studded with a multitude of sensors can be controlled more precisely, raising efficiency. And when operating environments are monitored continuously for hazards or when objects can take corrective action to avoid damage, risks and costs diminish. Companies that take advantage of these capabilities stand to gain against competitors that don't.

The widespread adoption of the Internet of Things will take time, but the time line is advancing thanks to improvements in underlying technologies. Advances in wireless networking technology and the greater standardization of communications protocols make it possible to collect data from these sensors almost anywhere at any time. Ever-smaller silicon chips for this purpose are gaining new capabilities, while costs, following the pattern of Moore's Law, are falling. Massive increases in storage and computing power, some of it available via cloud computing, make number crunching possible at very large scale and at declining cost.

Putting the Internet of Things to work: **Information and analysis**

Tracking behavior

Monitoring the behavior of persons, things, or data through space and time

Examples:
Presence-based advertising and payments based on locations of consumers

Inventory and supply chain monitoring and management

None of this is news to technology companies and those on the frontier of adoption. But as these technologies mature, the range of corporate deployments will increase. Now is the time for executives across all industries to structure their thoughts about the potential impact and opportunities likely to develop from the Internet of Things. We see six distinct types of emerging applications, which fall in two broad categories: first, information and analysis and, second, automation and control.

Information and analysis

As the new networks link data from products, company assets, or the operating environment, they will generate better information and analysis, which can enhance decision making significantly. Some organizations are starting to deploy these applications in targeted areas, while more radical and demanding uses are still in the conceptual or experimental stages.

1. Tracking behavior

When products are embedded with sensors, companies can track the movements of these products and even monitor interactions with them. Business models can be fine-tuned to take advantage of this behavioral data. Some insurance companies, for example, are offering to install location sensors in customers' cars. That allows these companies to base the price of policies on how a car is driven as well as where it travels. Pricing can be customized to the actual risks of operating a vehicle rather than based on proxies such as a driver's age, gender, or place of residence.

Or consider the possibilities when sensors and network connections are embedded in a rental car: it can be leased for short time spans to

Enhanced situational awareness

Achieving real-time awareness of physical environment

2

Example:
Sniper detection using direction of sound to locate shooters

registered members of a car service, rental centers become unnecessary, and each car's use can be optimized for higher revenues. Zipcar
has pioneered this model, and more established car rental companies are starting to follow. In retailing, sensors that note shoppers'
profile data (stored in their membership cards) can help close purchases by providing additional information or offering discounts at
the point of sale. Market leaders such as Tesco are at the forefront
of these uses.

In the business-to-business marketplace, one well-known application of the Internet of Things involves using sensors to track RFID (radio-
frequency identification) tags placed on products moving through
supply chains, thus improving inventory management while reducing
working capital and logistics costs. The range of possible uses for
tracking is expanding. In the aviation industry, sensor technologies are
spurring new business models. Manufacturers of jet engines retain
ownership of their products while charging airlines for the amount of
thrust used. Airplane manufacturers are building airframes with
networked sensors that send continuous data on product wear and
tear to their computers, allowing for proactive maintenance and
reducing unplanned downtime.

2. Enhanced situational awareness

Data from large numbers of sensors, deployed in infrastructure
(such as roads and buildings) or to report on environmental conditions
(including soil moisture, ocean currents, or weather), can give
decision makers a heightened awareness of real-time events, particularly when the sensors are used with advanced display or visualization technologies.

Security personnel, for instance, can use sensor networks that
combine video, audio, and vibration detectors to spot unauthorized

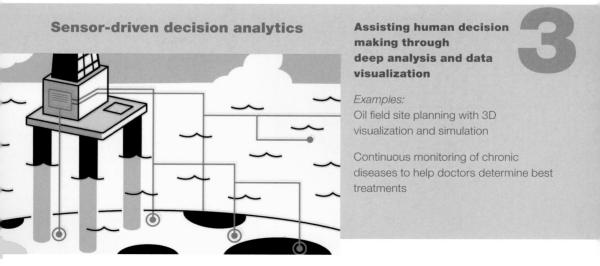

Sensor-driven decision analytics

Assisting human decision making through deep analysis and data visualization

3

Examples:
Oil field site planning with 3D visualization and simulation

Continuous monitoring of chronic diseases to help doctors determine best treatments

individuals who enter restricted areas. Some advanced security systems already use elements of these technologies, but more far-reaching applications are in the works as sensors become smaller and more powerful, and software systems more adept at analyzing and displaying captured information. Logistics managers for airlines and trucking lines already are tapping some early capabilities to get up-to-the-second knowledge of weather conditions, traffic patterns, and vehicle locations. In this way, these managers are increasing their ability to make constant routing adjustments that reduce congestion costs and increase a network's effective capacity. In another application, law-enforcement officers can get instantaneous data from sonic sensors that are able to pinpoint the location of gunfire.

3. Sensor-driven decision analytics

The Internet of Things also can support longer-range, more complex human planning and decision making. The technology requirements—tremendous storage and computing resources linked with advanced software systems that generate a variety of graphical displays for analyzing data—rise accordingly.

In the oil and gas industry, for instance, the next phase of exploration and development could rely on extensive sensor networks placed in the earth's crust to produce more accurate readings of the location, structure, and dimensions of potential fields than current data-driven methods allow. The payoff: lower development costs and improved oil flows.

As for retailing, some companies are studying ways to gather and process data from thousands of shoppers as they journey through stores. Sensor readings and videos note how long they linger at individual displays and record what they ultimately buy. Simulations based on this data will help to increase revenues by optimizing retail layouts.

In health care, sensors and data links offer possibilities for monitoring a patient's behavior and symptoms in real time and at relatively low cost, allowing physicians to better diagnose disease and prescribe tailored treatment regimens. Patients with chronic illnesses, for example, have been outfitted with sensors in a small number of health care trials currently under way, so that their conditions can be monitored continuously as they go about their daily activities. One such trial has enrolled patients with congestive heart failure. These patients are typically monitored only during periodic physician office visits for weight, blood pressure, and heart rate and rhythm. Sensors placed on the patient can now monitor many of these signs remotely and continuously, giving practitioners early warning of conditions that would otherwise lead to unplanned hospitalizations and expensive emergency care. Better management of congestive heart failure alone could reduce hospitalization and treatment costs by a billion dollars annually in the United States.

Automation and control

Making data the basis for automation and control means converting the data and analysis collected through the Internet of Things into instructions that feed back through the network to actuators that in turn modify processes. Closing the loop from data to automated applications can raise productivity, as systems that adjust automatically to complex situations make many human interventions unnecessary. Early adopters are ushering in relatively basic applications that provide a fairly immediate payoff. Advanced automated systems will be adopted by organizations as these technologies develop further.

1. Process optimization

The Internet of Things is opening new frontiers for improving processes. Some industries, such as chemical production, are installing legions of sensors to bring much greater granularity to monitoring. These sensors feed data to computers, which in turn analyze them and then send signals to actuators that adjust processes—for example, by modifying ingredient mixtures, temperatures, or pressures. Sensors and actuators can also be used to change the position of a physical object as it moves down an assembly line, ensuring that it arrives at machine tools in an optimum position (small deviations in the position of work in process can jam or even damage machine tools). This improved instrumentation, multiplied hundreds of times during an entire process, allows for major reductions in waste, energy costs, and human intervention.

In the pulp and paper industry, for example, the need for frequent manual temperature adjustments in lime kilns limits productivity gains. One company raised production 5 percent by using embedded temperature sensors whose data is used to automatically adjust a kiln

Putting the Internet of Things to work: **Automation and control**

Process optimization

Automated control of closed (self-contained) systems

1

Examples:
Maximization of lime kiln throughput via wireless sensors

Continuous, precise adjustments in manufacturing lines

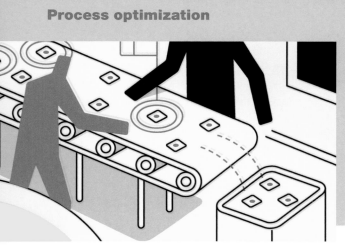

flame's shape and intensity. Reducing temperature variance to near
zero improved product quality and eliminated the need for frequent
operator intervention.

2. Optimized resource consumption

Networked sensors and automated feedback mechanisms can change
usage patterns for scarce resources, including energy and water,
often by enabling more dynamic pricing. Utilities such as Enel in Italy
and Pacific Gas and Electric (PG&E) in the United States, for example, are deploying "smart" meters that provide residential and industrial
customers with visual displays showing energy usage and the real-
time costs of providing it. (The traditional residential fixed-price-per-
kilowatt-hour billing masks the fact that the cost of producing energy
varies substantially throughout the day.) Based on time-of-use pricing
and better information residential consumers could shut down air
conditioners or delay running dishwashers during peak times. Commercial customers can shift energy-intensive processes and production away from high-priced periods of peak energy demand to low-
priced off-peak hours.

Data centers, which are among the fastest-growing segments of
global energy demand, are starting to adopt power-management techniques tied to information feedback. Power consumption is often
half of a typical facility's total lifetime cost, but most managers lack
a detailed view of energy consumption patterns. Getting such a
view isn't easy, since the energy usage of servers spikes at various times,
depending on workloads. Furthermore, many servers draw some
power 24/7 but are used mostly at minimal capacity, since they are
tied to specific operations. Manufacturers have developed sensors
that monitor each server's power use, employing software that bal-
ances computing loads and eliminates the need for underused

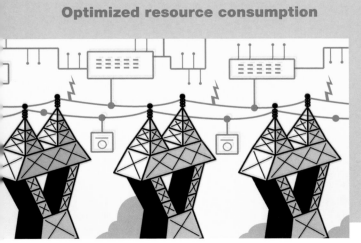

Optimized resource consumption

**Control of consumption
to optimize resource
use across network**

2

Examples:
Smart meters and energy grids that
match loads and generation capacity
in order to lower costs

Data-center management to optimize
energy, storage, and processor
utilization

servers and storage devices. Greenfield data centers already are adopting such technologies, which could become standard features of data center infrastructure within a few years.

3. Complex autonomous systems

The most demanding use of the Internet of Things involves the rapid, real-time sensing of unpredictable conditions and instantaneous responses guided by automated systems. This kind of machine decision making mimics human reactions, though at vastly enhanced performance levels. The automobile industry, for instance, is stepping up the development of systems that can detect imminent collisions and take evasive action. Certain basic applications, such as automatic braking systems, are available in high-end autos. The potential accident reduction savings flowing from wider deployment could surpass $100 billion annually. Some companies and research organizations are experimenting with a form of automotive autopilot for networked vehicles driven in coordinated patterns at highway speeds. This technology would reduce the number of "phantom jams" caused by small disturbances (such as suddenly illuminated brake lights) that cascade into traffic bottlenecks.

Scientists in other industries are testing swarms of robots that maintain facilities or clean up toxic waste, and systems under study in the defense sector would coordinate the movements of groups of unmanned aircraft. While such autonomous systems will be challenging to develop and perfect, they promise major gains in safety, risk, and costs. These experiments could also spur fresh thinking about how to tackle tasks in inhospitable physical environments (such as deep water, wars, and contaminated areas) that are difficult or dangerous for humans.

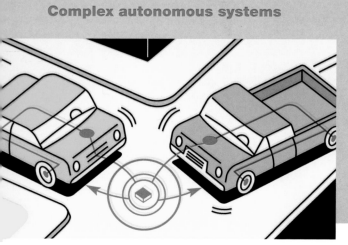

Complex autonomous systems

Automated control in open environments with great uncertainty

Examples:
Collision avoidance systems to sense objects and automatically apply brake

Clean up of hazardous materials through the use of swarms of robots

What comes next?

The Internet of Things has great promise, yet business, policy, and technical challenges must be tackled before these systems are widely embraced. Early adopters will need to prove that the new sensor-driven business models create superior value. Industry groups and government regulators should study rules on data privacy and data security, particularly for uses that touch on sensitive consumer information. Legal liability frameworks for the bad decisions of automated systems will have to be established by governments, companies, and risk analysts, in consort with insurers. On the technology side, the cost of sensors and actuators must fall to levels that will spark widespread use. Networking technologies and the standards that support them must evolve to the point where data can flow freely among sensors, computers, and actuators. Software to aggregate and analyze data, as well as graphic display techniques, must improve to the point where huge volumes of data can be absorbed by human decision makers or synthesized to guide automated systems more appropriately.

Within companies, big changes in information patterns will have implications for organizational structures, as well as for the way decisions are made, operations are managed, and processes are conceived. Product development, for example, will need to reflect far greater possibilities for capturing and analyzing information.

Companies can begin taking steps now to position themselves for these changes by using the new technologies to optimize business processes in which traditional approaches have not brought satisfactory returns. Energy consumption efficiency and process optimization are good early targets. Experiments with the emerging technologies should be conducted in development labs and in small-scale pilot trials, and established companies can seek partnerships with innovative technology suppliers creating Internet-of-Things capabilities for target industries. o

Related articles on mckinseyquarterly.com

Eight technology trends to watch

How to make Web 2.0 work

The authors wish to thank their McKinsey colleagues Naveen Sastry, James Manyika, and Jacques Bughin for their substantial contributions to this article.

We welcome your comments on this article. Please send them to quarterly_comments@mckinsey.com.

The new Japanese consumer

Brian Salsberg

The attitudes and behavior of Japanese consumers are shifting dramatically, presenting opportunities and challenges for companies in the world's second-largest retail market.

Seductive shelves piled with goods lure shoppers to a big-box retailer in Japan, where the company hopes to popularize deep-discount, bulk-purchase retailing.

After decades of behaving differently, Japanese consumers suddenly look a lot like their counterparts in Europe and the United States. Celebrated for their willingness to pay for quality and convenience and usually uninterested in cheaper products, Japanese consumers are now flocking to discount and online retailers. Sales of relatively affordable private-label foods have increased dramatically, and many consumers, despite small living spaces, are buying in bulk. Instead of eating out, people are entertaining at home. Workers are even packing their own lunches, sparking the nickname *bento-danshi*, or "box-lunch man".

This fundamental shift in the attitudes and behavior of Japanese consumers seems likely to persist, irrespective of any economic recovery. That's because the change stems not just from the recent downturn but also from deep-seated factors ranging from the digital revolution to the emergence of a less materialistic younger generation. An examination of the strategies of leading Japanese and multinational companies, along with interviews with more than two dozen executives of the most significant retail and consumer industry players, shows how consumers are changing and why. It also suggests the kinds of moves—such as rethinking relationships with customers and becoming more flexible about sales channels—that businesses must take to seize the opportunities created by Japan's new normal.

Brian Salsberg is a principal in McKinsey's Tokyo office.

How Japanese consumers are changing

Japanese consumers have long been both distinctive and reassuringly predictable. Unlike their counterparts in Europe and the United States, they eschewed low-priced goods, preferring high-end department stores and pricier regional supermarkets. They were willing to pay high prices for quality products, and their love of brands sparked the emergence of a mass-luxury market where owning expensive, exclusive products seemed essential rather than aspirational. This combination helped boost the country's retail sales to an estimated ¥135 trillion ($1.48 trillion) in 2008, second only to the United States. Yet Japan's consumers are rapidly changing, in four primary ways.

Hunting for value

Japanese consumers are reducing costs and questioning their famous inclination to pay for convenience: a September 2009 MyVoice Internet survey found that 37 percent had cut overall spending, while 53 percent declared themselves more likely to "spend time to save money" rather than "spend money to save time." In apparel, high-end department stores concerned about the vanishing shopper have started leasing space within their stores to value-focused competitors such as casual-clothing chains Uniqlo and Forever 21, hoping that this will revive customer traffic. Japan's leading skin care companies are more aggressively introducing lower-priced products. Luxury-goods companies are watching a decade of growth disappear, with year-on-year sales declines of 10 to 30 percent.

What's more, sales of private-label products are booming. Experience in many North American and Western European markets suggests that once people switch to private brands, they rarely change back. Japan is in the early stages of this transition: until recently, the private-label penetration rate was just 4 percent, compared with the global average of 20 percent.[1] Japan's largest retailer, Seven & I, which operates 7-Eleven convenience stores and Ito-Yokado general-merchandising stores, expects private-label sales to grow by about 60 percent, to ¥320 billion, this fiscal year.

Spending more time at home

The Japanese used to spend little time at home, as a result of factors such as long work hours and small living quarters. Yet almost 50 percent of a representative sample of consumers across a range of age groups and geographies are now spending somewhat or significantly more time there. The suddenness of this behavioral change has prompted a term for it: *sugomori*, or "chicks in the nest." In fact, a September 2009 MyVoice Internet survey found that the top four ways people chose to spend their days off were surfing the Internet, watching television or

[1] *Private Label Trends, Update 2009*, Planet Retail, January 2009.

The growing stay-at-home segment has earned its own nickname: *sugomori*—'chicks in the nest.'

Compared with 1 or 2 years ago, how much time are you spending at home?
% of respondents (n = 3,003)

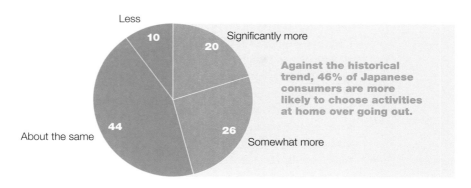

Source: Internet survey of Japanese consumers conducted for McKinsey, Nov 2009

reading the newspaper, sitting around the house, or listening to music. "I've seen people staying in more," said Ernest Higa, CEO of Higa Industries, which operates Domino's Pizza in Japan. "They're not going out, because of the economic crisis."

Buying products differently

Japanese consumers are changing not only what they buy but also how they buy it. Long given to shopping near their homes, they are now more willing to travel. They are also deserting department stores in unprecedented numbers, preferring to spend their time in malls and stand-alone specialty shops. Asked by a March 2009 MyVoice Internet survey to explain their defection from department stores, they cited expensive products, "annoying staff," and an "inability to shop at my own pace." Consumers are favoring venues that satisfy needs beyond shopping, such as eating and entertainment.

Online shopping is central to both the economizing and the nesting trends. While Japan has one of the world's highest broadband penetration rates, it has lagged behind developed markets such as United Kingdom and the United States in the willingness of its consumers to shop online. Many explanations have been advanced for this peculiarity: Japanese consumers love the physical shopping experience; mobile-phone screens are too small; the density of retail establishments means that online shopping has less of a convenience advantage; credit card penetration is low.

Whatever the root causes, Japan has shrugged off its reluctance: according to an April 2009 MyVoice Internet survey, more than 50 percent of consumers are buying more online than they were just 12 months ago. "Mobile technologies are empowering consumers to make smarter decisions about what they buy," said Duncan Orrell-Jones, senior vice president and general manager of Disney Interactive Media (Asia-Pacific). The total online market for physical goods (excluding ticket sales and electronic downloads of media such as music, movies, and software) is estimated to be nearly $30 billion, compared with only $1.3 billion in 1999.[2] When Domino's, for example, launched an Internet-based home-delivery service, in 2004, the company's first long-term internal target was to have 5 percent of home-delivery orders placed through it. To Higa's surprise, "over 35 percent of our sales today are through the Internet."

It's worth underscoring the tight relationship between online shopping and broader shifts in consumer behavior. In a consensus-driven society where individual choice and expression have historically been frowned upon, the ability to browse products, compare prices, and make purchases relatively anonymously is creating new attitudes and empowering consumers. An interesting example is health care, where

[2] Sales figure for 1999 from Jason Dedrick and Kenneth L. Kraemer, "Japan E-commerce report," Center for Research on Information Technology and Organizations, University of California, Irvine, December 2000.

The Japanese Internet retail market will grow to at least $50 billion by 2015.

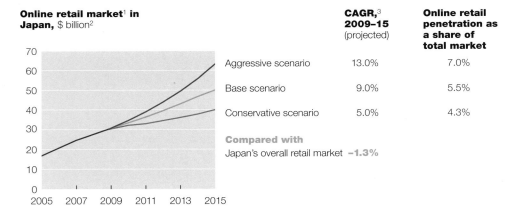

Online retail market[1] in Japan, $ billion[2]

	CAGR,[3] 2009–15 (projected)	Online retail penetration as a share of total market
Aggressive scenario	13.0%	7.0%
Base scenario	9.0%	5.5%
Conservative scenario	5.0%	4.3%

Compared with
Japan's overall retail market **−1.3%**

[1]Excluding sales of tickets and electronic downloads of media such as music, movies, and software.
[2]Average exchange rate in 2009: $1 = ¥100.
[3]Compound annual growth rate.

Source: Euromonitor International, Dec 2009; "Current and expected landscape of mail order/e-commerce business in 2008-2009," Fuji-Keizai; "Research on utilization in Japan 2008," Japanese Ministry of Economy, Trade, and Industry (METI); McKinsey analysis

the Japanese have traditionally been deferential to authority figures
such as physicians. Yet according to a nationwide January 2009 Nomura
Research Institute survey, 89 percent of Japan's people are somewhat
or very interested in managing their own health care decisions.

Being health- and environment-conscious

Japan has always been perceived as one of the world's healthiest
societies, thanks to a combination of lifestyle, diet, and genetics, and
Japanese consumers are increasingly conscious of their health.
A September 2009 MyVoice Internet survey suggests that spending on
health, sports, and recreation, for example, has held up better than
virtually any other retail category. One effect of the greater interest of
the Japanese in directing their own health care has been the growing popularity of drugstores, which have been Japan's fastest-growing
retail channel since 2000: store numbers have increased by 4 percent and sales by 8 percent.

Environmental consciousness has been emerging for some time.
A survey conducted last year by the global advertising agency J. Walter
Thompson found that 51 percent of Japanese consumers are somewhat or much more focused on the environment than they were a year
ago; only 7 percent were less focused. A November 2009 McKinsey
survey found that 84 percent of the respondents preferred to buy envi-
ronmentally friendly everyday consumer products, and that preference is translating directly into business success. Consider, for example,
Coca-Cola's I LOHAS (Lifestyles of Health and Sustainability) water,
whose selling points include a reduced carbon footprint: bottles are
made from 12 grams of recyclable PET[3] plastic (rather than the
standard 26 grams) that can be twisted and compressed when recycled.
I LOHAS is also bottled locally, reducing transportation costs. Less
than 12 months after launch, it has become Japan's top-selling brand
of single-serve bottled water.

Despite such success stories, Japanese consumers, like their counterparts in many other markets, have hard-nosed attitudes about paying for
green goods and services. Just 16 percent of Japanese respondents to
a recent McKinsey survey expressed a willingness to pay more for them.

Why behavior is changing

Three factors are contributing to these trends—first and most obvi-
ously, the current economic downturn. Just as European and US consumers have become more frugal, so have the Japanese. There's
also a longer-term trend at work: Japan's economy has been relatively
weak for nearly two decades. The changes that has wrought—such

[3] Polyethylene terephthalate, a thermoplastic polymer resin.

as the disappearance of life-long jobs and the increase in part-time and temporary labor—is fuelling consumer anxiety. The most recent (October 2009) J. Walter Thompson AnxietyIndex suggests that 90 percent of Japanese consumers feel anxious or nervous, the highest rate of any country in the world. While some money-saving behavioral changes (spending less, buying through different channels, going out less) stem from the downturn, it has in all likelihood primarily accelerated changes under way for some time.

Related to this anxiety is a second factor: the emergence of a new generation with radically different attitudes. This generation—people in their 20s—has grown up through Japan's difficult economic climate, never knowing the boom times the two previous ones experienced. Its lifestyle has prompted the nickname the *hodo-hodo zoku*, or "so-so folks" (or, even worse, "slackers" or "herbivore men"). Many shun corporate life and material possessions and are more pessimistic and more likely to be unemployed than their elders.

Related articles on mckinseyquarterly.com

Japan's luxury shoppers move on

How the recession has changed US consumer behavior

Consumer electronics gets back to basics

These young men and women present a challenge to marketers. As the CEO of a leading sports-apparel company in Japan recently said, "For the first time, we have a generation of consumers that aren't at all persuaded by what the professional athletes are wearing. We need a fundamental rethink of how to approach this next generation." In addition, these consumers tend to be more willing to spend money on services than products and on technology than other goods. In December 2008, when a goo Research Internet survey asked Japanese women aged 20 to 26 which products (of any kind) exhibited superior design, for instance, four of the top five were made by Apple, and just a handful of luxury goods made the list.

A final factor driving the change in attitudes and behavior is a series of small, largely unrelated regulatory actions. In March 2009, for example,

Japan's government reduced the maximum freeway toll on weekends to ¥1,000 regardless of the distance traveled—a huge discount that encouraged trips outside Tokyo to big-box discounters and large-format retailers such as Costco and Ikea. Other examples include regulations allowing the wider sale of over-the-counter drugs; a mandate that all employees over the age of 40 (about 50 million people) take a test to determine whether they are at risk for conditions such as diabetes and high blood pressure and, if they are, requiring them to exercise and diet; and recent changes to reduce underage smoking. The Japanese government has also pushed to increase awareness of and access to health remedies, in part to address the challenge of paying to treat these conditions.

• • •

All these changes add up to a new playing field for domestic and international companies. Because Japanese consumer behavior is shifting closer to that of shoppers in Europe and the United States, retailers and manufacturers can look to those markets for guidance. For starters, they should place greater emphasis on generating and maintaining customer loyalty and be willing to experiment with new store formats that better match the way consumers now shop. Companies also should embrace online shoppers for any product, from the high to the low end, given their increasing numbers. "Marketers must begin to think about digital marketing as an extension of the product itself and not just an extra piece of media," said one Japan-based chief marketing officer of a major consumer products multinational.

The author would like to acknowledge the contributions of Tomoko Hibino-Niitani and Todd Guild to this article.

We welcome your comments on this article. Please send them to quarterly_comments@ mckinsey.com.

The shift to value has already generated some unlikely winners—McDonald's has become Japan's biggest-selling restaurant chain—and helped companies that have traditionally struggled to gain traction. Ikea has become Japan's second-biggest furniture retailer. Costco membership is at an all-time high. Wal-Mart Stores' Japanese operation, Seiyu, reported its best financial results since entering the market. Amazon.com is doing remarkably well. Non-Japanese players are enjoying unprecedented success, and local manufacturers and retailers must respond proactively. Some are thriving—furniture group Nitori has excelled in a down market, as has online retailer Rakuten—but others may need to seek mergers to reduce operational costs and remain competitive, or partner with major retailers to bypass wholesalers and middlemen.

One thing is certain: the world's second-largest consumer market is changing as Japanese consumers increasingly resemble their Western peers. For Western companies that have long regarded selling in Japan as not only different but also difficult, this may be welcome news indeed. ○

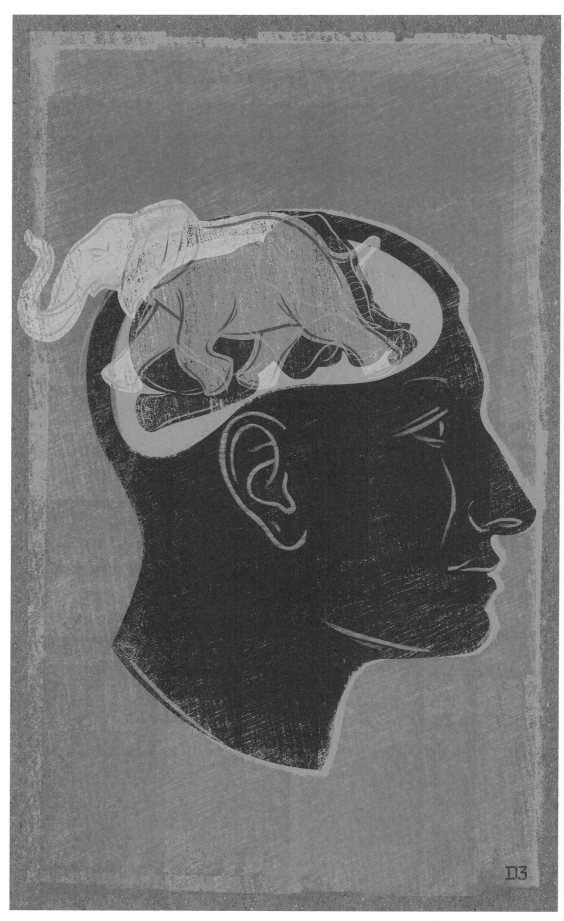

Making the emotional case for change

An interview with Chip Heath

In conversation and in excerpts from his recent book, a leading expert on organizational behavior explains why change often stalls and how top executives can use psychology to keep it going.

Chip and Dan Heath's new book, *Switch: How to Change Things When Change Is Hard*, shows how managers can catalyze change more effectively by drawing on an enormous body of research from psychologists on how the brain works. In *Switch*'s first chapter, the authors report that they hope most of all to help "people who don't have scads of authority or resources." But the book's ideas have enormous relevance for senior executives as well. In this interview with McKinsey's Allen Webb, Heath interprets *Switch* for denizens of the C-suite. Supporting the interview are two case examples excerpted from the book.

The *Quarterly*: *Could you please quickly summarize the core ideas in* Switch *for the benefit of those who have not yet read it?*

Chip Heath: The core idea is that there are two sides to the way human beings think about any issue. There's the rational, analytical, problem-solving side of our brains, which may think, "I need to eat less." But there's an emotional side that's addicted to impulse or comfortable routines, and that side wants a cookie. At work, the rational side may say that the company needs to go in a different direction. But the emotional side is comfortable with the old ways of thinking and selling, and it has great anxiety about whether the company can change successfully.

My favorite metaphor for this dynamic comes from the psychologist Jonathan Haidt, who talks about a human riding atop an elephant.[1] The Rider represents our analytical, planning side. The Rider decides, "I need to go somewhere, here's the direction I want to go," and sets off. But it's the Elephant, the emotional side, that's providing the power. The Rider can try to lead the Elephant, but in any direct contest of wills the Elephant is going to win—it has a six-ton advantage. So part of achieving change, in either our lives or in organizations, is aligning both sides of the brain by pointing out the direction for the Rider but also motivating the Elephant to undertake the journey. Of course, the Path the Elephant walks down matters too. High-ranking executives can shape that Path, that environment, and make the journey easier even when the Elephant is less motivated.[2]

The *Quarterly*: *In helping companies to work through these conflicts and smooth the road to change, how useful is a senior executive's formal power?*

Chip Heath: The Rider–Elephant conflict may be a reason not to press too hard on formal levers. It's not enough for people to intellectually understand that an organization must start moving in a different strategic direction. People need to be motivated.

Our typical way of communicating speaks primarily—and in a lot of cases almost exclusively—to the Rider. It builds an intellectual case

[1] *The Happiness Hypothesis: Putting Ancient Wisdom to the Test of Modern Science*, London: William Heinemann, 2006.
[2] In *Switch*, the words *Rider*, *Elephant*, and *Path* represent characters in the mental play that the book describes.

Chip Heath

Vital statistics
Married,
with 2 children

Education
Graduated with
BS in industrial
engineering in
1986 from Texas
A&M University

Received PhD
in psychology in
1991 from
Stanford University

Career highlights
Currently a professor of organizational behavior at Stanford Graduate School of Business

Fast facts
Coauthor with his brother Dan Heath of *Made to Stick: Why Some Ideas Survive and Others Die*, which has been translated into 27 languages; has published research in such academic publications as *Cognitive Psychology, Organizational Behavior and Human Decision Processes*, and the *Quarterly Journal of Economics*, and his research has been reviewed in publications including *Scientific American*, the *Financial Times*, the *Washington Post*, and *Vanity Fair*

Serves on editorial board of *Stanford Social Innovation Review*

for change and relies on formal authority. In government, legislators have formal authority to change the rules of the system. The US Congress once changed the national speed limit to 55 miles an hour, for example. Did that automatically change behavior? As a parent, does formal power change the behavior of your teenagers?

It's not enough to show intellectually that we need to change and then to decree what those changes will be. If it were, a lot more organizations would succeed in making strategic shifts. Formal power is tremendously useful, but if we *start* by wielding it we probably haven't aligned the Rider and the Elephant. And if we rely *only* on the formal levers of power to lead, we may get too far ahead of people—they understand that they must change, but the motivation hasn't kicked in.

The *Quarterly*: *What's an example of the kind of formal power you think executives mistakenly exercise and an alternative that might be more effective?*

Chip Heath: Consider how change initiatives are typically rolled out. In many organizations, a change initiative consists of 35 slides in a PowerPoint deck analyzing the reasons for change. There's nothing in the deck that helps employees believe that "We're the kind of people who can successfully make this change."

GE overcame this problem when they started talking about "ecomagination." CEO Jeff Immelt said, "There's a broad social trend toward finding more sustainable ways of doing business, and if we can take advantage of that, we will be well-positioned for the future." GE did a green audit, looking for places where they already had industry-leading green products, and started highlighting those existing products for employees. One was an LED[3] lighting system that produces great light with 10 percent of the electricity used by other systems. GE then said, "We're the kind of people who can succeed in this new business environment that's more and more focused on sustainability." That motivates the Elephant.

The *Quarterly*: *In* Switch*, you use the term "bright spots" to describe internal success stories like GE's LED system. Could you say a bit more about the power of bright spots?*

Chip Heath: Many companies try change themselves by benchmarking other organizations and borrowing their procedures or practices. The irony of benchmarking is that we're essentially telling organizations to be more like GE or Apple or Nike. As Dev Patnaik, the author of *Wired to Care*,[4] said to me one time, we know this doesn't work on a personal

---

[3] Light-emitting diode, a semiconductor light source.
[4] *Wired to Care: How Companies Prosper When They Create Widespread Empathy*, Upper Saddle River, NJ: FT Press, 2009.

level: we resist when members of our families say, "Be more like your brother." The principle of bright spots is that you shouldn't try to be more like Apple; you should try to be more like yourself at your best moments. Think about what you've done in the past, or what you're doing now, that has worked tremendously well.

People have a tendency, especially in a change situation, to focus on the negative. Lots of research supports this negative focus—for example, if you ask sports fans what happened over the weekend, they dwell on the games their favorite teams lost. Companies too focus on the problems and not the bright spots.

I won't say there's no value in benchmarking. But if you believe that organizations differ in their cultures, capabilities, and structures, there's something fundamentally odd about saying that you want to be more like another company that has a very different culture, structure, and set of capabilities. At the very least, the idea of looking to your own bright spots is a useful addition to your tool kit.

Excerpt from *Switch*: Inventing an identity

Brasilata—a $170 million Brazilian producer of steel cans—actually *invented* the identity that became the engine of its success. Can manufacturing is a relatively mature industry—not much growth or excitement. But Brasilata defies the boring, stuck-in-its-ways stereotype. In fact, it has one of the best reputations for *innovation* of any company in Latin America.

How does a metal can company become known as an innovator? Brasilata's founders were inspired by the philosophy of Japanese car manufacturers like Honda and Toyota, which empowered their frontline employees to take ownership of their work. In 1987, the founders launched their own employee-innovation program.

A new identity was its core. Employees became known as "inventors," and new hires were asked to sign an "innovation contract." This wasn't just feel-good language. Employees were challenged to be on the lookout for ideas on how to create better products, improve production processes, and cut costs. Systems were developed that made it easy to submit ideas. The program succeeded beyond reasonable expectations. In 2008, a total of 134,846 ideas were submitted—an average of 145.2 ideas per inventor!

These suggestions often led to new products. In late 2008, for instance, the company came up with a new approach for a steel can designed to carry flammable or otherwise dangerous

The *Quarterly*: *What's your view of the notion that change is easier when you have a "burning platform" from which to motivate it?*

Chip Heath: That is one of the silliest pieces of business jargon. The idea of the burning platform is that people only change when they're scared. But fear, as an emotion, creates tunnel vision. Police officers call this "weapon focus": crime victims can often give great descriptions of the weapon, but nothing about whether the assailant was tall or short or had facial hair, because they focus on what evoked their fear.

That kind of tunnel vision is devastating in times of change. If you're doing everything basically right and you just need to improve execution, you can scare people and they'll execute better and faster. But that's not true of most change situations, where you need to be doing something new. Fear is the worst motivator here because it makes people work harder at what they did in the past.

The *Quarterly*: *In* Switch*, you talk a lot about "identity." Why is that important?*

liquids. To meet UN standards, such cans must withstand a drop from about four feet. Most companies had solved this problem by thickening the metal layers, which used up more raw material. And even the reinforced cans were prone to split if they landed on an edge. Brasilata's inventors suggested a new design, inspired by car bumpers that collapse on impact. The new cans deformed slightly on impact, reducing stress on the critical seam. They resisted falls better while also reducing the amount of steel in the can.

Inventors have also led the company through emergencies. In 2001, a severe energy crisis forced Brazil's government to give businesses a strict quota of electricity. In response,

Brasilata's employees dreamed up hundreds of power-saving ideas. Within a few weeks, Brasilata's energy consumption had fallen by 35 percent, reducing it below quota, so the company could resell the extra energy.

Let's remember something: this inventor identity, which has fueled the company's business success and employee satisfaction, was made up. None of Brasilata's employees was born an inventor. This identity was introduced to them, and they decided it was a mantle worth wearing—a source of pride and strength.

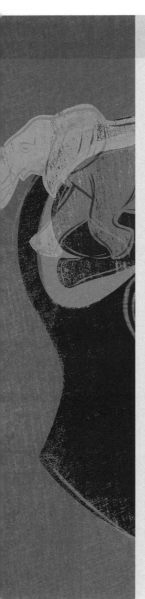

Excerpt from *Switch*: Making bad behavior impossible

Rackspace hosts Internet sites for other companies, and it has won an armload of trade awards for service. But it wasn't always so customer friendly. Originally, says the company's founder, Graham Weston, Rackspace had a "denial of service" business model. Customer service interactions were viewed as costs to be minimized—the more roadblocks that could be erected to keep the phone from ringing, the better profits would be.

Then, in the autumn of 1999, came The Call. A customer tried to telephone Rackspace for support. He pressed 5 to get help, but instead he got a voice mail that said, "Feel free to leave a voice mail here, but we don't check it very often, so you're better off sending us an e-mail." He grudgingly sent one, but Rackspace never answered it. After a few more of these irritating cycles, the customer was furious, and with a bit of legwork he tracked down Graham Weston at the office of a real-estate business Weston owned. Weston promised to investigate.

He reviewed the long, increasingly angry chain of e-mails. "Something hit me," said Weston. "It was something

that we could do very easily that he couldn't do. So the question in my mind was, 'Why are we not serving the customer happily?'" Weston knew his team couldn't sustain a business based on dodging its customers. "We made a 180-degree turn."

Weston hired David Bryce as head of customer support. At his first meeting with the team, Bryce announced that Rackspace would transform itself from a company that dreaded customer support into a company that was passionate about it. He posted an aspirational banner on the wall: "Rackspace Gives Fanatical Support." The phrase stuck immediately.

This was just talk, of course, but there was action to back it up. Weston started by overhauling the company's business model. Providing great service would inevitably cost more, and if Rackspace offered both premium service and cutting-edge technology it would have to set prices too high. So, remarkably, Weston pushed for the company to become technologically dull. "We don't want to be on the bleeding edge of technology. We believe in standardization. We want a

Chip Heath: My Stanford colleague Jim March says there are two very different kinds of logic for making decisions. One is the logic of consequences. We're great in business at changing behavior by changing consequences. If we want customers to buy more, we lower prices. If we want salespeople to sell more, we increase their bonuses. But the second kind of logic is the logic of identity. Many of the most profound decisions we make in life are made because of identity, not consequences. When our newborn child cries at night, we don't undertake a net pres-

narrow focus; these are the things we do, and these are things we don't do," he said—clear direction for the Rider.

Perhaps the most dramatic change Weston and Bryce made was also the simplest. Rackspace, like all hosting companies, had a call-queuing system. ("Your call is important to us. Please press 1 for recorded tips that don't address your problem, 5 to leave us a message we won't return, and 8 to repeat these options.") The call queue is perhaps the most basic customer support tool. Weston threw it out.

"When a customer calls, that means they need our help, and we've got to answer the telephone," he said. Without the queuing system, there was no safety net; the phone would keep ringing until somebody picked it up. To Weston, this was a critical symbol of the service ethic—when customers have a problem, we should deal with it when it's convenient for them, not us. Weston made it *impossible* to dodge the customer.

Subsequently, the company launched the "straightjacket awards," including actual straightjackets as trophies, which were presented to employees who'd been so fanatical about service they'd become downright insane. (That's an identity appeal for the Elephant: *we are zealots—that's what makes us special.*) Not coincidentally, in 2008 Rackspace was named, for the second time, among the companies in *Fortune*'s list of Best Places to Work.

By 2007, Rackspace was talking to customers three times a week, on average. The focus on service paid off. In 2001, the company became the first Internet-hosting firm to turn a profit, and over the next six years it *averaged* 58 percent annual growth. By 2008, it had passed AT&T as the industry's highest-grossing company.

What transformed the character of Rackspace's customer service people? Nothing. They were just operating in a new environment. The old behavior (ignoring customers) had become harder and the new behavior (serving customers) easier. What looks like a character problem is often an environment problem.

ent value analysis of how much more valuable an hour of sleep would be. We get up because we are a committed mother or father.

That's useful in business, especially in a change situation: if we can harness the power of identity, it helps motivate the Elephant to undertake a long, arduous journey. In a change situation, you want creativity and flexibility—and that's more likely to come from identity than from consequences. Consequence-based logic is great at narrowing people's focus, but it can backfire for the same reason. If you give people incentives to sell a lot of mortgages, for instance, they will do so. But they're not necessarily selling the right mortgages to the right people.

Most successful companies have a distinctive identity in our minds. I can picture the identity of a Wal-Mart or a Southwest or an IBM employee. I have a harder time picturing the identities of some of their competitors. Intel recently has been running a national ad campaign that features its own employees. It's called "Our rock stars aren't like your rock stars." Ajay Bhatt, one of the coinventors of USB, is shown walking into a company canteen and being surrounded by adoring employees. The point is that what they value at Intel may be different from what's valued in the outside world, but if you're the next Ajay Bhatt, you want to work for Intel, where your talents will be respected. Another great example of a company that motivates employees by giving them a sense of identity is Brasilata.

The *Quarterly*: *How can senior executives create appropriate identities?*

Chip Heath: They don't have to be invented from whole cloth, because, again, you can build on bright spots. For example, when Lou Gerstner came to IBM it had a long tradition of selling "big iron," or large mainframe computers. But there was also a division selling solutions that might or might not involve IBM hardware. Its employees had an identity as problem solvers for customers. Gerstner seized on that existing expertise and rolled it out as IBM's strategy.

As a top leader, you want to use your platform to celebrate people, like Ajay Bhatt, who create and sustain your company's identity. At Brasilata, they tell stories about great innovations from frontline employees. In identity-based logic, we think about how "people like us" behave in order to uphold an identity. Celebrating case studies of success is exactly what a company should do.

The *Quarterly*: *You said earlier that the Path the Elephant walks down matters. Could you elaborate?*

Chip Heath: One company we studied was Rackspace, an Internet-hosting company. Graham Weston, its chairman, used his power to clear away a barrier in the Path—a call-queuing system that made employees respond to customers in lazy ways. He also used his power to simplify the strategy by moving away from cutting-edge technology. Especially for a technology company, that seemed scary. But Weston said that we want plain-vanilla technology because we're going to excel in service.

Lots of research in behavioral economics shows that too much choice is paralyzing. Especially in a change situation, a big part of freeing up the creativity needed for change may be simplifying internal processes. Once Weston became clear about his strategy, he simplified the engineering world at Rackspace and raised the prominence of the customer service people.

The *Quarterly*: *Sometimes change is harder. How do leaders create an environment where people view failures along the road as learning opportunities?*

Chip Heath: In any organizational-change situation, there will be setbacks, times of confusion. In the change plans of big organizations, there is a planning phase and an execution phase, but no slot in the middle for a wandering-around-in-the-dark phase. We pretend we'll jump straight from planning to brilliant execution. As a top leader, you should make people realize that there will be difficulties, but that those difficulties aren't going to prevent ultimate success.

Related articles on mckinseyquarterly.com

Corporate transformation under pressure

The irrational side of change management

The psychology of change management

In *Switch*, we discuss the design firm IDEO, which deals with this problem a lot because it often tries to train entrenched bureaucratic organizations to design more innovative products. An IDEO designer sketched a mood chart predicting how employees feel at different phases of a project. It's a U-shaped curve with a peak labeled "hope" at the start and a peak labeled "confidence" at the end. In between is a negative valley labeled "insight." In IDEO's experience, there is always a moment when an innovation team feels demoralized. Yet eventually an answer will appear, so if the team keeps working through that frustration, things will get better. Every manager in a change process should steal IDEO's chart because every change process goes through that same sequence of mood changes.

We welcome your comments on this article. Please send them to quarterly_comments@ mckinsey.com.

The *Quarterly*: *What messages do you want to leave with senior executives who are seeking to catalyze change?*

Chip Heath: Pay attention to creating an emotional case for change, not just an analytical one. Scale up bright-spot successes. And use your power as a top leader to smooth the path to change. Your people are ready to step up to the plate, but if systems or procedures are getting in the way of change, you are the one with the power to eliminate them. o

 **Picture This**

Counting the world's unbanked

Percentage of total adult population who do not use formal or semiformal financial services

- ▬ 0–25%
- ▬ 26–50%
- ▬ 51–75%
- ▬ 76–100%

▬ **Estimates** used to calculate regional averages

High-income OECD countries
60 million adults
(Members of Organisation for Economic Co-operation and Development)

8%

Latin America
250 million adults

65%

Total
2,455 million adults

53%

Alberto Chaia, Tony Goland, and Robert Schiff

Alberto Chaia is a principal in McKinsey's Mexico City office, Tony Goland is a director in the Washington, DC, office, and Robert Schiff is a consultant in the New York office.

Fully 2.5 billion of the world's adults don't use formal banks or semiformal microfinance institutions to save or borrow money, our research finds. Nearly 2.2 billion of these unserved adults live in Africa, Asia, Latin America, and the Middle East. Unserved, however, does not mean unservable.

The microfinance movement, for example, has long helped expand credit use among the world's poor—reaching more than 150 million clients in 2008 alone.[1] Similarly, we find that of the approximately 1.2 billion adults in Africa, Asia, and the Middle East who use formal or semiformal credit or

Source: McKinsey research conducted in partnership with the Financial Access Initiative (a consortium of researchers at New York University, Harvard, Yale, and Innovations for Poverty Action); we relied on financial usage data from Patrick Honohan, "Cross-country variation in household access to financial services," *Journal of Banking & Finance*, 2008, Volume 32, Number 11, pp. 2493–500.

The unbanked are not unservable

Yet serving adults who live on less than $5 a day is not only possible at scale— to a large degree, it is already happening.

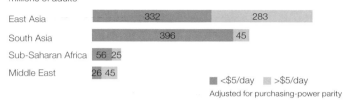

Adults who use formal or semiformal financial services, millions of adults

	<$5/day	>$5/day
East Asia	332	283
South Asia	396	45
Sub-Saharan Africa	56	25
Middle East	26	45

Adjusted for purchasing-power parity

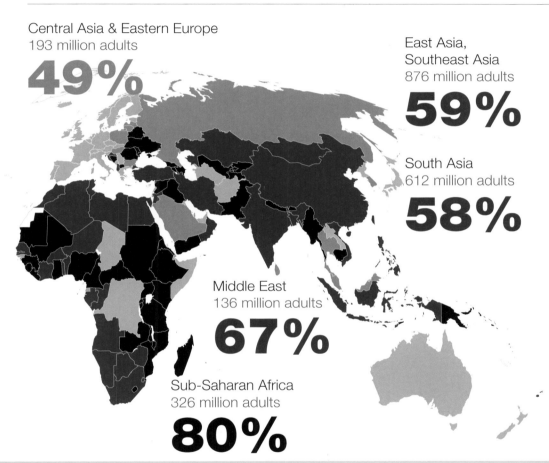

Central Asia & Eastern Europe
193 million adults
49%

East Asia, Southeast Asia
876 million adults
59%

South Asia
612 million adults
58%

Middle East
136 million adults
67%

Sub-Saharan Africa
326 million adults
80%

savings products, about 800 million live on less than $5 a day. Large unserved populations represent opportunities for institutions that are able to offer an innovative range of high-quality, affordable financial products and services. Moreover, with the right financial education and support to make good choices, lower-income consumers will benefit from credit, savings, insurance, and payments products that help them invest in economic opportunities, better manage their money, reduce risks, and plan for the future. O

[1]According to the Microcredit Summit Campaign, a leading advocacy group.

 To read the full report, *Half the World is Unbanked*, visit sso.mckinsey.com/unbanked.

Applied insight

Tools, techniques, and frameworks for managers

Using behavioral science to improve the customer experience

John DeVine and Keith Gilson

By guiding the design of customer interactions, the principles of behavioral science offer a simple, low-cost route to improved customer satisfaction.

John DeVine is a principal in McKinsey's Miami office, and Keith Gilson is a consultant in the Toronto office.

Service operations seem a natural setting for the ideas of behavioral science. Every year, companies have thousands, even millions, of interactions with human beings (also known as customers), whose perceptions of an interaction, behavioral scientists tell us, are influenced powerfully by considerations such as its sequence of painful and pleasurable experiences. Companies care deeply about the quality of those interactions and invest heavily in effective Web sites and in responsive, simplified call centers.

Yet the application of behavioral science to service operations seems spotty at best. Its principles have been implemented by relatively few

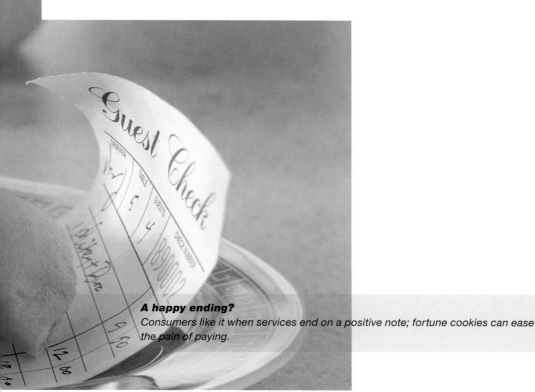

A happy ending?
Consumers like it when services end on a positive note; fortune cookies can ease the pain of paying.

companies, such as the telecommunications business, which found that giving customers some control over their service interactions by allowing them to schedule field service visits at specific times could make them more satisfied, even when they had to wait a week or longer. Many more companies ignore what makes people tick. Banks, for example, often disturb the customer experience by altering the menus on ATMs or the interactive-voice-response (IVR) systems in call centers. They fail to recognize the psychological discomfort customers experience when faced with unexpected changes.

Likewise, for every restaurant that surrounds a bill's arrival with a succession of complementary desserts—thereby capitalizing on the customer's preference for service encounters that end positively—there are a lot of call centers that ignore the importance of a strong finish. Indeed, many companies actively work against one by placing so much emphasis on average handling times that they inadvertently encourage agents to end a call once its main business is complete, leaving customers with memories of brusque treatment.

It doesn't have to be this way. Academics such as Professor Richard Chase at the University of Southern California's Marshall School of Business have used research on how people form opinions about their experiences to design actual services. In a 2001 *Harvard Business Review* article,[1] Chase and his team even laid out principles for managers to consider when designing any customer interaction. Get bad experiences over with early, so that customers focus on the more positive subsequent elements of the interaction. Break up pleasure but combine pain for your customers, so that the pleasant parts of the interaction form a stronger part of their recollections. Finish strong, as the final elements of the interaction will stick in the customers' memory. Give them choice, so they feel more in control of the interaction. And let them stick to their habits rather than force them to endure the discomfort and disorientation of unexpected change.

Here we review the experience of an insurance company that used those principles to improve its customers' satisfaction significantly, with no incremental costs or

[1] For more, see Richard B. Chase and Sriram Dasu, "Want to perfect your company's service? Use behavioral science," *Harvard Business Review*, June 2001, Volume 79, Number 6, pp. 78—84.

Results of applying behavioral science to long-term illness treatment

Improved: Patient satisfaction, patient motivation, nurses' job satisfaction

Unchanged: Costs, number of calls per day, average length of call

Nurses made regular, scheduled calls to patients in the health-management program.

fundamental changes in people or infrastructure. A systematic approach like this one is needed to counteract the natural tendency of service operations to focus on the needs of IT systems and work flows, not to mention the preferences of employees, managers, and service providers, largely ignoring the way customers perceive their service interactions. If companies in a broad range of service industries—including banking, telecommunications, and retailing—applied a rigorous approach, they would reap significant economic benefits, ranging from reduced churn to greater cross-selling to additional customer referrals.

In practice

Executives at a leading North American health insurer sought to help patients manage their treatment programs for serious long-term illnesses, such as diabetes or congestive heart failure. Conditions like these are difficult to manage because treatment is often protracted and outcomes can depend on the patients' willingness to make significant lifestyle changes.

Patients participating in an experimental health-management program received regular, scheduled calls from a team of nurses over a period of several months. The calls

were aimed to deliver additional support to patients undergoing long-term treatment by helping them understand the available options and stick to their treatment regimes, as well as by reinforcing lifestyle changes recommended by their doctors. Improved compliance helps insurers too, as better outcomes reduce the overall cost of treatment.

In the past, the clinical-treatment program for each patient had determined the content of such calls, and the company used what it considered to be a tried-and-true method for managing them. Team members had received guidelines on the objectives of the calls and used a checklist to sequence discussions with customers.

To see if this approach could be improved, the company divided the nurses into two groups—approximately 20 in a pilot group and another 20 in a control one—and began applying a behavioral-science lens to the interactions of the former to test different versions of the call structure. Postcall surveys measured the customers' satisfaction with each call and with the company. Key customer and operational metrics (including sign-up rates) helped estimate the financial impact. The pilot team used behavioral-science principles throughout the interactions.

Lessons from the trenches

1
Get bad experiences over with early

The team identified difficult issues— for example, the forthcoming lapse of certain insurance benefits or the need to transfer from one facility to another—and moved them to the start of the call. It also set up a later phase built around constructive coaching from the nurses on how to deal with the issues raised earlier. In addition, general questions that were likely to make patients uncomfortable (about current pain levels, smoking habits, eating patterns, and alcohol consumption, for instance) were moved from the end of the call to the beginning.

2
Break up pleasure and combine pain

By combining the most challenging elements of a call in its first phase, the health-management team could focus on positive aspects during the rest of it. The team found that patients responded very positively to coaching by nurses, so there was an effort to ensure that coaching on multiple topics was an explicit part of every phase of the call. A nurse might, for example, discuss the next treatment steps, how the patient could take advantage of all covered benefits, and ways of minimizing out-of-pocket expenses. There was also an effort to resolve all possible issues within a call and to transfer it to other groups only as a last resort.

3
Finish strongly

The conclusion of the health-management calls was scripted to finish on a positive note by emphasizing the tangible insurance benefits available to patients and, where medically appropriate, the likelihood of a successful outcome to the agreed-upon action plan. At the end of a program lasting several months, with calls taking place every month or so, patients received a final call from their health-management nurse. This call ended by celebrating their progress, reviewing the goals they had met, and summarizing the positive steps they had taken to achieve those goals.

By breaking down frontline transactions and rebuilding them with behavioral and experiential principles, many other service industries could systematically achieve rapid, measurable improvements in customer satisfaction

4 Give customers choice

The company made an effort to give customers explicit choice on three critical elements: the type of treatment plan, which facilities to visit and which doctors to see, and the timing of future calls. In each area, the nurse was guided to tell the customer, "You have a choice; let me give you some options."

Customers explicitly had the right to make the ultimate decision, though the outcome may have been limited or strongly suggested—for example, "Hospital A is closest to your home, but B is only 15 minutes further away, and it has a specialist unit with a great track record at treating your condition."

5 Let customers stick to their habits

In many situations, it was important for patients to change their lifestyles—say, by eating different foods, consuming less alcohol, or exercising. To encourage patients to make these changes while minimizing the discomfort they generated, nurses introduced them gradually over a series of calls. Dietary changes might be discussed initially, for instance, followed by encouragement to begin exercise. The nurses also tried to reframe the patients' perceptions of the severity of the changes by comparing them with more unfavorable alternatives: for example, "instead of eliminating your favorite foods altogether, why not just try picking low-fat varieties next time you are in the store."

The team also worked to ensure that the calls themselves became a positive habit for the patients. This approach gave them the option of having the same nurse on follow-up and promoted a consistent approach for every call, so that they became used to the interactions.

Results

The effect of the changes was significant. Patients in the test group reported an average satisfaction level seven percentage points higher than that of patients in the control group—for calls with the same basic content. These patients' satisfaction levels with the company was on average eight percentage points higher than that of the control group. More important, patients in the test group were on average five percentage points more likely to say that the calls had motivated them to make positive changes in their behavior.

Notably, the program didn't significantly affect the company's costs or change key operational metrics, such as the length of a call or the number of calls a day. Moreover, test group nurses reported an average level of job satisfaction higher than that of the control group nurses. Finally, the impact was rapid. Most of the increase in the satisfaction levels of the test group patients happened within two weeks.

Many other service industries could benefit from a similar approach. By breaking down frontline transactions and rebuilding them with behavioral and experiential principles, companies could systematically achieve rapid, measurable improvements in customer satisfaction. **o**

Harness the power of a default option

Make a product's cost less painful

Position your preferred option carefully

Don't overwhelm consumers with choice

A marketer's guide to behavioral economics

Ned Welch

Marketers have been applying behavioral economics— often unknowingly—for years. A more systematic approach can unlock significant value.

Ned Welch is a consultant in McKinsey's Toronto office.

Long before behavioral economics had a name, marketers were using it. "Three for the price of two" offers and extended-payment layaway plans became widespread because they worked—not because marketers had run scientific studies showing that people prefer a supposedly free incentive to an equivalent price discount or that people often behave irrationally when thinking about future consequences. Yet despite marketing's inadvertent leadership in using principles of behavioral economics, few companies use them in a systematic way. In this article, we highlight four practical techniques that should be part of every marketer's tool kit.

1. Make a product's cost less painful

In almost every purchasing decision, consumers have the option to do nothing: they can always save their money for another day. That's why the marketer's task is not just to beat competitors but also to persuade shoppers to part with their money in the first place. In economic principle, the pain of payment should be identical for every dollar we spend. According to marketing practice, however, many factors influence the way consumers value a dollar and how much pain they feel upon spending it.

Retailers know that allowing consumers to delay payment can

dramatically increase their willingness to buy. One reason delayed payments work is perfectly logical: the time value of money makes future payments less costly than immediate ones. But there is a second, less rational basis for this phenomenon. Payments, like all losses, are viscerally unpleasant. But emotions experienced in the present—*now*—are especially important. Even small delays in payment can soften the immediate sting of parting with your money and remove an important barrier to purchase.

Another way to minimize the pain of payment is to understand the ways "mental accounting" affects decision making. Consumers use different mental accounts for money they obtain from different sources rather than treating every dollar they own equally, as economists believe they do, or should. Commonly observed mental accounts include windfall gains, pocket money, income, and savings. Windfall gains and pocket money are usually the easiest for consumers to spend. Income is less easy to relinquish, and savings the most difficult of all.

Technology creates new frontiers for harnessing mental accounting to benefit both consumers and marketers. A credit card marketer, for instance, could offer a Web-based or mobile-device application that gives consumers real-time feedback on spending against predefined budget and revenue categories—green, say, for below budget, red for over budget, and so on. The budget-conscious consumer is likely to find value in such accounts (although they are not strictly rational) and to concentrate spending on a card that makes use of them. This would not only increase the issuer's interchange fees and financing income but also improve the issuer's view of its customers' overall financial situation. Finally, of course, such an application would make a genuine contribution to these consumers' desire to live within their means.

2. Harness the power of a default option

The evidence is overwhelming that presenting one option as a default increases the chance it will be chosen. Defaults—what you get if you don't actively make a choice—work partly by instilling a perception of ownership before any purchase takes place, because the pleasure we derive from gains is less intense than the pain from equivalent losses. When we're "given" something by default, it becomes more valued than it would have been otherwise—and we are more loath to part with it.

Savvy marketers can harness these principles. An Italian telecom company, for example, increased the acceptance rate of an offer made to customers when they called to cancel their service. Originally, a script informed them that they would receive 100 free calls if they kept their plan. The script was reworded to say, "We have already credited your account with 100 calls— how could you use those?" Many customers did not want to give up free talk time they felt they already owned.

Defaults work best when decision makers are too indifferent, confused, or conflicted to consider their options. That principle is particularly relevant in a world that's increasingly awash with choices—a default eliminates the need to make a decision. The default, however, must also be a good choice for most people. Attempting to mislead customers will ultimately backfire by breeding distrust.

3. Don't overwhelm consumers with choice

When a default option isn't possible, marketers must be wary of generating "choice overload," which makes consumers less likely to purchase. In a classic field experiment, some grocery store shoppers were offered the chance to taste a selection of 24 jams, while others were offered only 6. The greater variety drew more shoppers to sample the jams, but few made a purchase. By contrast, although fewer consumers stopped to taste the 6 jams on offer, sales from this group were more than five times higher.[1]

Large in-store assortments work against marketers in at least two ways. First, these choices make consumers work harder to find their preferred option, a potential barrier to purchase. Second, large assortments increase the likelihood that each choice will become imbued with a "negative halo"—a heightened awareness that every option requires you to forgo desirable features available in some other product. Reducing the number of

[1]Sheena S. Iyengar and Mark R. Lepper, "When choice is demotivating: Can one desire too much of a good thing?" *Journal of Personality and Social Psychology*, 2000, Volume 79, Number 6, pp. 995–1006. The study is also cited in Sheena Iyenar's new book, *The Art of Choosing* (Twelve Publishing, 2010).

The jam test: When shoppers were offered only six jams to sample, the purchase rate was more than five times higher.

6 jam varieties

Number of people who sampled jams

24 jam varieties

Number of people who eventually purchased jam

options makes people likelier not only to reach a decision but also to feel more satisfied with their choice.

4. Position your preferred option carefully

Economists assume that everything has a price: your willingness to pay may be higher than mine, but each of us has a maximum price we'd be willing to pay. How marketers position a product, though, can change the equation. Consider the experience of the jewelry store owner whose consignment of turquoise jewelry wasn't selling. Displaying it more prominently didn't achieve anything, nor did increased efforts by her sales staff. Exasperated, she gave her sales manager instructions to mark the lot down "x½" and departed on a buying trip. On her return, she found that the manager misread the note and had mistakenly doubled the price of the items—and sold the lot.[2] In this case, shoppers almost certainly didn't base their purchases on an absolute maximum price. Instead, they made inferences from the price about the jewelry's quality, which generated a context-specific willingness to pay.

The power of this kind of relative positioning explains why marketers sometimes benefit from offering a few clearly inferior options. Even if they don't sell, they may increase sales of slightly better products the store really wants to move. Similarly, many restaurants find that the second-most-expensive bottle of wine is very popular—and so is the second-cheapest. Customers who buy the former feel they are getting something special but not going over the top. Those who buy the latter feel they are getting a bargain but not

being cheap. Sony found the same thing with headphones: consumers buy them at a given price if there is a more expensive option—but not if they are the most expensive option on offer.

Another way to position choices relates not to the products a company offers but to the way it displays them. Our research suggests, for instance, that ice cream shoppers in grocery stores look at the brand first, flavor second, and price last. Organizing supermarket aisles according to way consumers prefer to buy specific products makes customers both happier *and* less likely to base their purchase decisions on price— allowing retailers to sell higher-priced, higher-margin products. (This explains why aisles are rarely organized by price.) For thermostats, by contrast, people generally start with price, then function, and finally brand. The merchandise layout should therefore be quite different.

Marketers have long been aware that irrationality helps shape consumer behavior. Behavioral economics can make that irrationality more predictable. Understanding exactly how small changes to the details of an offer can influence the way people react to it is crucial to unlocking significant value—often at very low cost. o

The author would like to acknowledge their colleague Micah May's contributions to this article.

[2] Robert B. Cialdini, *Influence: Science and Practice*, New York: HarperCollins, 1993.

Using knowledge brokering to improve business processes

Corey Billington and Rhoda Davidson

New applications of open-innovation principles allow progressive companies to enhance not only their products but also their core internal business processes.

Corey Billington is a professor of operations management and procurement at the International Institute for Management Development (IMD), in Lausanne, Switzerland. Rhoda Davidson, a program manager at IMD, is an alumnus of McKinsey's London office.

Savvy product makers have long viewed existing ideas as inspiration for new ones—recall how in the late 1990s the designers of the SpinBrush famously adapted the technology from a battery-operated, spinning lollipop to create an inexpensive, electric toothbrush for P&G. More recently, we've observed some fifty teams at ten multinational companies apply the same "find, don't invent" mentality to process redesign by looking outside their walls to effectively tap a rich vein of useful—and unexpected—know-how from a variety of industries, disciplines, and contexts. By using this old approach, called "knowledge brokering,"[1] in new ways these companies are creating novel solutions to a mix of strategic, operational, and organizational problems.

Understandably, some senior executives will be skeptical of (yet another) theoretical-sounding application of open innovation. Finding and encouraging outsiders to collaborate, for example, might seem complicated, costly, or risky. It is none of these. The rise of Web-based social- and professional-networking sites such as Facebook and LinkedIn make accessible the collective know-how of millions

[1] The term *knowledge brokering* was coined by Andy Hargadon and Robert Sutton to describe companies, spanning multiple markets and technology domains, that move innovations around from business to business. We recommend these authors' seminal article on the topic: "Building an innovation factory," *Harvard Business Review*, July 2004, Volume 78, Number 3, pp. 157–66.

© Robert Caplin

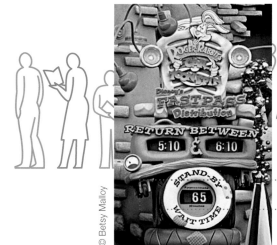

© Betsy Malloy

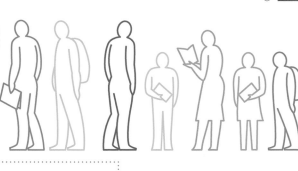

of managers, thus allowing project teams to quickly locate a surprising range of knowledge by using their own extended networks. Moreover, most experts are happy to talk for free. This is largely human nature (people like talking about themselves). Also the speaker, or knowledge broker, typically gains new insight into their own experiences simply by organizing their thoughts and verbalizing them. Finally, the processes being discussed are usually common knowledge within the broker's industry and therefore don't represent an intellectual-property risk.

Consider, for example, the commercial bank in the United Kingdom that faced frequent complaints from customers about long lines in its branches. The bank's project team began by identifying several promising sources of brokers including amusement parks, where customers spend considerable time in lines; supermarkets, where razor-thin margins force companies to devote a lot of energy to the problem; and department stores, where seasonal fluctuations in customer levels are common.

Next, the team used its social and professional networks to identify relevant brokers. These included a traffic-circulation-planning expert, a Disney theme park manager, and a manager from the UK grocer Tesco.

A bank in the United Kingdom that had problems with long lines identified Disney, grocery stores, and traffic planners as possible knowledge brokers.

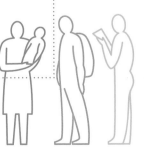

 For the full report, see *Using knowledge brokering to improve business processes*, available free of charge on mckinsey.com.

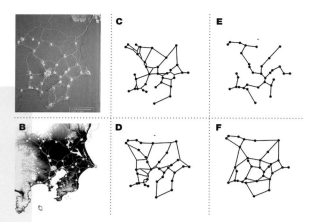

C

E

B

D

F

The insights gained from these brokers proved invaluable. The bank, for example, ultimately designed a successful ticketing option inspired by Disney's Fastpass, which gives the company's amusement park patrons the option of avoiding a long wait for a ride by scheduling one during a specific window of time later on. Another "a-ha" moment was learning from Disney managers about how customers become irritated when they can see the "full horror" of a long line. Consequently, the bank redesigned its teller windows in a circle, so that customers would be less able to see the whole length of a line or to become annoyed if some of the teller stations are unstaffed. From Tesco, the bank learned about "dynamic queuing," which led to the creation of a customized system for using back-office staffers to substitute for tellers when the foot traffic in a branch exceeds certain thresholds.

Of course, many sources of expertise are available through more traditional means: Suppliers, potential suppliers, customers, and professional networks all offer rich sources of expertise. Suppliers, in particular, are typically delighted to help. When a large manufacturer of office equipment, for example, was redesigning a process to develop stronger relationships with its indirect channel partners, it found that its IT enterprise systems partner was eager to share information. Likewise, when a UK subsidiary of a major European utility was reinforcing its in-house shared-services strategy, for example, it gathered useful perspectives from companies interested in gaining outsourcing business.

The key is seeking out a wide range of different sources—and not necessarily from world-class companies or even experts. Any manager or other experienced person can be a good source of information if he or she has more experience than the seeker at the process in question. Moreover, many useful brokers come from outside conventional business environments. Professionals such as doctors, lawyers, dentists, and administrators of nongovernmental organizations (NGOs) can make highly effective brokers.

Some companies find even more unusual sources for insight. For example, an engineering-services firm we studied found it had more projects than it could handle, and although it was thriving, the company feared it might lose customers if it couldn't immediately meet their needs. By speaking with managers of popular night clubs and highly rated restaurants, the engineering firm learned how to say "no" more diplomatically, and without burning bridges. To be sure, not all senior executives might be comfortable reaching quite this far outside their walls for insights. However, by tapping into a wide variety of knowledge sources and combining outside insights with internal ones, companies can improve their business processes, while better preparing for an increasingly networked world where success depends not just on *what* employees know but *whom* they know. o

A new way to measure word-of-mouth marketing

Jacques Bughin, Jonathan Doogan, and Ole Jørgen Vetvik

Assessing its impact as well as its volume will help companies take better advantage of buzz.

Jacques Bughin is a director in McKinsey's Brussels office, Jonathan Doogan is an associate principal in the London office, and Ole Vetvik is a principal in the Oslo office.

Consumers have always valued opinions expressed directly to them. Marketers may spend millions of dollars on elaborately conceived advertising campaigns, yet often what really makes up a consumer's mind is not only simple but also free: a word-of-mouth recommendation from a trusted source. As consumers overwhelmed by product choices tune out the ever-growing barrage of traditional marketing, word of mouth cuts through the noise quickly and effectively.

Indeed, word of mouth[1] is the primary factor behind 20 to 50 percent of all purchasing decisions. Its influence is greatest when con-sumers are buying a product for the first time or when the product is relatively expensive, which tends to make people conduct more research, seek more opinions, and consider their options longer than they otherwise would. And its influence will probably grow: the digital revolution has amplified and accelerated its reach, for word of mouth is no longer an act of intimate, one-on-one communication. Today, it also operates on a one-to-many basis: product reviews are posted online and opinions disseminated through social networks. Some customers even create Web sites or blogs to praise or punish brands.

[1] The term *word of mouth,* as used in this article, means consumer-to-consumer communication with no economic incentives. The sender may, however, reap social gratifications or rewards.

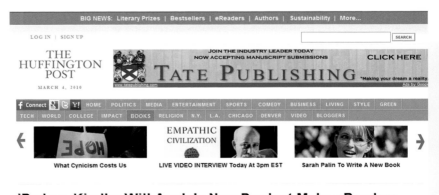

As online communities increase in size, number, and character, marketers have come to recognize word of mouth's growing importance. But measuring and managing it is far from easy. A starting point for many has been counting the number of recommendations and dissuasions for a given product. There's an appealing power and simplicity to this approach, but also a challenge: it's difficult for marketers to take into account differences in the power of different kinds of word-of-mouth messages. After all, a consumer is significantly more likely to buy a product as a result of a recommendation made by a family member than by a stranger. These two kinds of recommendations constitute a single message, yet the difference in their impact on the receiver's behavior is immense. In fact, our research shows that a high-impact recommendation— from a trusted friend conveying a relevant message, for example—is up to 50 times more likely to trigger a purchase than is a low-impact recommendation.

To assess the impact of these different kinds of recommendations, we developed a way to calculate what we call word-of-mouth "equity"—an index of a brand's power to generate messages that influence the consumer's decision to purchase. Word-of-mouth equity represents the average sales impact of a brand message multiplied by the number of word-of-mouth messages. By looking at both their impact and their volume, this measurement allows a marketer to accurately test their effect on sales and market share for brands and for companies as a whole. That impact—in other words, the ability of any one word-of-mouth recommendation or dissuasion to change behavior—reflects what is said, who says it, and where. It also varies by product category.

Word-of-mouth equity measures the impact, as well as the volume, of consumers' recommendations.

Effect of word-of-mouth messages on company brand   ● High impact ● Low impact

| **Volume** | **x** | **Impact** | **=** | **Word-of-mouth equity** |

Few messages

Many messages

Network: Where are they talking?
- ➕ Close/trusted
- ➖ Large/dispersed

Sender: Who is talking?
- ➕ Influential
- ➖ Noninfluential

Message content: What are they saying?
- ➕ Relevant key buying factor for consumer
- ➖ Irrelevant key buying factor for consumer

Message source: What is the trigger?
- ➕ Consumer's own experience with product or service
- ➖ Trigger not based on personal experience, eg, hearsay

Strong equity, for example:

Few

BUT . . .
- ● Close/trusted
- ● Influential
- ● Favorable buying factor
- ● Consumer's own experience

Marketers tend to build campaigns around emotional positioning, yet we found that consumers actually tend to talk—and generate buzz—about functional messages.

What's said—the content of a message—is the primary driver of word-of-mouth impact.

Across most product categories, we found that a message must address important product or service features if it is to influence consumer decisions. In the mobile-phone category, for example, design is more important than battery life. In skin care, packaging and ingredients create more powerful word of mouth than emotional messages about how a product makes people feel. Marketers tend to build campaigns around emotional positioning, yet we found that consumers actually tend to talk—and generate buzz—about functional messages.

The second critical driver is the identity of the person who sends a message.

About 8 to 10 percent of consumers are what we call *influentials*, whose common factor is trust and competence: the word-of-mouth receiver must trust the sender and believe that he or she really knows the product or service in question. Our research does not identify a homogenous group of consumers who are influential across categories: consumers who know cars might influence car buyers but not consumers shopping for beauty products. Influentials typically generate three times more word-of-mouth messages than non-influentials, and each message has four times more impact on a recipient's purchasing decision. About 1 percent of these people are digital influentials—most notably bloggers—with disproportionate power.

Finally, the environment where word of mouth circulates is crucial to the power of messages.

Typically, messages passed within tight, trusted networks have less reach but greater impact than those circulated through dispersed communities—in part because there's usually a high correlation between people whose opinions we trust and the members of networks we most value. That's why old-fashioned kitchen table recommendations and their online equivalents remain so important. After all, a person with 300 friends on Facebook may happily ignore the advice of 290 of them. It's the small, close-knit network of trusted friends that has the real influence. **o**

Rediscovering the art of selling

Josh Leibowitz

Even after researching products on their own, many customers still enter stores undecided about what to buy. For retailers, that's an opportunity.

Josh Leibowitz is a principal in McKinsey's Miami office.

Retailers as far back as the legendary pioneer Marshall Field once focused intensely on clinching sales once customers walked into stores. But recently, the industry has been missing opportunities to make sales. New technologies, extensive retailer Web sites, mobile-shopping tools, and in-store Internet kiosks have separated customers from sales associates. Content to let consumers research products independently, many retailers have been reducing in-store sales staff and eliminating commission-based models. This approach has resulted in lower costs, but it has also reduced incentives for those left on the floor to make sales.

Many retailers assume that customers walk into stores for purely transactional purposes: they know what they want and just need to buy it. Yet McKinsey research indicates that as many as 40 percent of customers remain open to persuasion once they enter a store,[1] despite undertaking extensive product research, reading online reviews, and comparing prices on their own. Retailers that fail to have knowledgeable staff on hand to help customers make decisions, or even to create arresting in-store visual marketing materials, are losing sale after potential sale. More than ever, retailers need a sales-driven mind-set focused on having the right number of sales staff; ensuring those staff are knowledgeable, well-trained, and motivated to sell; and providing the right in-store experience for customers.

[1] See David Court, Dave Elzinga, Susan Mulder, and Ole Jørgen Vetvik, "The consumer decision journey," mckinseyquarterly.com, June 2009.

Bolstering the sales staff

Many retail executives argue they can't afford to provide high-value sales help. Simple arithmetic suggests they can't afford *not* to. It's true that adding frontline staff that can sell effectively is costly and takes time, and we're not suggesting a return to an old-fashioned, expensive, labor-intensive sales system. But there's a powerful and straightforward business case for investing in frontline sales staff: when done correctly, adding salespeople offers one of the more attractive payback opportunities in retail.

Consider the case of home electronics sold through discount stores— the ultimate self-help format, where consumers typically undertake product comparisons independently before ultimately going to a store to make a purchase. With an average selling price of $200 and an average gross margin of 10 percent, or $20 per sale, the cost of hiring a good salesperson is recouped by selling just one additional product per hour on the floor. When the profit margin from up-selling or cross-selling accessories is added, just one additional sale every two hours is needed. At one self-help apparel company, for example, providing extra sales assistance during select hours led to a conversion rate increase of 9 percent, driving fitting-room use 37 percent higher and recouping the cost of the extra human help within an average of 10 to 15 minutes during normal selling hours.

Building the right frontline sales force

Watch skilled salespeople at work and you soon realize that while selling is an art that can be approached in a variety of ways, it boils down to four basic steps: open, ask for needs, demonstrate, and close. Surprisingly few frontline sales associates know these steps well, and fewer do all four consistently. At one retailer, for example, we found that associates failed to ask to close the sale 86 percent of the time. Having staff that understand and enjoy the sales process is paramount, and that means attracting the right employees, training them effectively, and rewarding them appropriately.

Effective sellers share common traits: they are motivated by helping customers, have extroverted personalities, and are passionate about their work. Our research indicates that, at most, 45 percent of frontline employees across multiple retailing sectors have the personality and attributes to be effective sellers.[2] Retailers need to redesign the way they hire and deploy staff into selling roles to attract employees with the personality and attributes required to succeed. In addition, we found that few retailers provide training with the specificity and quality to effectively support sales associates in their mission to sell more. That leaves even natural salespeople often unable to answer basic questions about their products from potential customers who are increasingly informed (in some categories, more than 75 percent appear in the store having done extensive independent research).

[2] The survey was completed in August 2008 and received responses from 1,675 frontline employees across eight retail sub-sectors: apparel and footwear, department stores, discount stores and warehouse clubs, drugstores, groceries, large specialty stores, off-price retailers, and small specialty retailers.

Improving the in-store experience

Better visual merchandising can make a big difference in helping consumers make certain buying decisions, accelerating the payback on frontline staff. Consider one self-help retailer that simplified its point-of-sale signage for digital cameras to make comparing products easier for both consumers and sales staff. Rather than using techno-logical jargon such as megapixels and zoom sizes, the retailer instead used "photo-enlargement sizes" and "distance to picture object." Memory cards emphasized the number of photographs a card could hold, rather than describing them in gigabytes. Because sales staff could use the visual displays as a way to sell products to customers without having to memorize technical details, they were more confident and achieved more sales per hour.

Examining the way consumers make decisions also makes a difference. At one leading personal-bath-care chain, for example, executives realized that people pre-ferred to shop by "scent" rather than "function"—they preferred all vanilla products in one area, rather than all shampoos in one area and all soaps in another. Reorga-nizing the entire merchandising layout from a function-based to a scent-based display resulted in increased category sales, as customers bought multiple products with the same scent, rather than just one. It was a simple but effective change reflecting how consumers actually shop. Paying attention to these kinds of customer behaviors remains invaluable, despite the unprecedented access to product information, reviews, and prices that consumers have online. o

Missed opportunity?

Enduring Ideas

Classic McKinsey
frameworks
that continue to
inform management
thinking

The strategic-control map

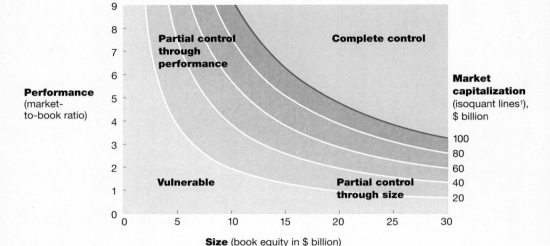

[1] An isoquant line is drawn through those points in a graph where equal quantity of output is achieved though quantities of component inputs change.

The strategic-control map uses market capitalization dynamics to help companies identify their biggest opportunities and threats, as well as to boost their odds of hunting for acquisition targets rather than being hunted themselves. Developed in 1996 by McKinsey consultants Vijay D'Silva, Bill Fallon, and Asheet Mehta, the framework tracks the relationship between the two dimensions of market capitalization by plotting a company's size (measured by book value) against its performance for shareholders (measured by market-to-book ratio).

Companies mapped in this way fall into four groups, each with its own strategic imperatives. The large, high-performing companies in the upper right are the least likely to be acquisition targets. Their challenge is to maintain a strong position by pursuing fresh opportunities without watering down returns. Companies in the lower left, the most vulnerable to takeover, must improve the performance of their existing businesses or reinvest in others and divest losers. Companies in the upper left often possess proprietary knowledge or skills that enable them to earn high returns from intangibles. They can largely maintain strategic control unless their performance drops. Finally, if large companies in the lower right don't improve their performance, they could become inviting cost-consolidation targets for even larger, better-performing industry leaders.

The enduring power of the framework lies in its ability to visualize how changes in market capitalization affect the market for strategic control. You can see at a glance which companies in a given industry are likely to be acquirers and which are likely to be acquired. ○